The Creative
Table

The Creative Table

Inspired Recipes that Nourish, Gather and Unite

by MICHELLE M. M^cGRATH

Design by Rachel Turner, Visual Solutions

Photography by Michelle M. McGrath

First trade edition published in 2020
by Michelle M. McGrath, Scituate, MA
mcgrathpr.com
with Amazon Kindle Direct Publishing

Printed in the United States of America

ISBN 978-0-578-78634-6

5 4 3 2

Acknowledgements

To my three children, now adults, with a deep love for the gifts with which you have each endowed my life, relatedly the opportunity to cultivate and hone my cooking skills across the last quarter century, nourishing your world. May these recipes be the foundation of a culinary legacy with which your future cooking adventures ignite.

To my dear friends Elaine, Anne, Gail and Su who offered countless words of encouragement and their keen eyes and hearts to the editing and solutions that resulted in this book's success.

To my business venture partner Dan, for his unfailing production support and willingness to serve as taste tester for almost anything concocted in my kitchen.

To my parents, and the many family, friends, neighbors, acquaintances and sometimes strangers, taste testers or otherwise, that often or only once allowed me to fortify your life in some tiny way by doing what I love — making kitchen creations and sharing the resulting meals and treats as nourishment and kindness.

Contents

Introduction

While navigating the waters of life's diverse stages — raising children, steering a thriving business, celebrating family — cooking and baking have endured as my anchor. At every turn of the compass, the simple act of preparing food in my kitchen has calmed every storm. Elevating all-things-culinary to the level of adventure was initially sparked by nourishing family and friends at my table. As is my nature, my inner-artist eventually stepped in...

STRONGLY INFLUENCED BY NEW ENGLAND ROOTS...

inspiring the creation of original and adapted dishes that have stayed the course — the vessel frame for this cookbook.

Arriving at my half century milestone set my mind on an introspective course. I recollected those cherished years I spent at home as a stay-at-home mom to my three wonderful children, and I realized the importance of preserving their childhood memories through tastes, sights and smells. Together we've cherished many holidays and marked life's milestones. We've filled the tables of school bake sales, provided meals in support of those in need and gathered beloved friends and family in a myriad of celebrations. Food has served our family as a memorable treasure, a bond for all the senses, an enduring sentiment.

Today, the kitchen perseveres as the epicenter of my artistry. Aspirations to hone my skills as a baker and home cook have evolved into a passion to nourish those I love. Cooking and baking have emerged as my sustainable art form, my source of escape, fulfillment and satisfaction. It keeps my mind sharp, centered and inventive; our table constantly evolving as the hub of life.

The great pandemic pause of 2020 brought with it the unexpected gift of opportunity. This treasured quiet time gave me the nudge I needed to gather 40 years of hand scribbled recipes into a culinary memory book. I refined instructions, carefully crafting this one-of-a-kind vessel, chronicled from the underside of the hull to the tip of the mast. The resulting recipe collection is as representative of a love for fresh ingredients and creativity as it is the melting pot of culture that is anchored in the community and vitality of New England. Images are sourced from my own lens, reflecting the coastal region we call home, throughout the four seasons and in the gardens, as colorful as a kitchen palette.

I've enjoyed testing these waters with friends, family and my children, who kindly bolster my endeavors with endless support. Memorable conversations yielding vivid reactions inspired this cookbook's completion in just 50 days from its inception. In retrospect, it seems the contents were practically already written within the experiences we've shared, recounted in each indelible anecdote, every delicious memory.

Spend time in the kitchen with these recipes, and I guarantee those you share them with will feel nurtured and loved. I hope you seize every opportunity to gather and create your own treasured memories. Raise the mast in earnest, center your compass and take sail, steering those you love back to your creative table, time and time again.

With love and gratitude,

Michelle M. McGrath

Appetizers

Garlic Dill Refrigerator Pickles

Bacon and Bleu Crostini

A favorite vehicle for spontaneous recipe creation is a quick peek in the cabinets and refrigerator, especially when company is soon on their way! This concoction started as a last-minute nosh and quickly rose to festive favorite status at first bite.

Makes 16 servings

Preheat oven to 350° F. Place baguette slices on a baking sheet and bake for 5-8 minutes until lightly toasted, turning once during baking. Remove baking sheet from oven, leaving oven up to temperature. Rub each hot baguette slice with the cut side of the garlic cloves, discard remaining garlic.

Meanwhile, in a small bowl, blend half of the bleu cheese, the cream cheese, spices, salt and pepper until smooth and evenly combined. Spread each baguette slice thinly with fig jam, then top with the cheese mixture. Sprinkle evenly with crumbled bacon and remaining blue cheese. Return the baking sheet to oven and bake until the cheese mixture is melted and slightly puffed, about 6 more minutes. Top crostini with minced chives or scallions, and serve warm.

INGREDIENTS:

1 French baguette,
cut diagonally into 16 - ½" slices

2 large cloves garlic, halved, skin removed

4 ounces bleu cheese, crumbled, divided

4 ounces cream cheese, at room temperature

1 teaspoon fresh dill
or ½ teaspoon dried dill weed

1 teaspoon fresh thyme
or ½ teaspoon dried thyme

¼ teaspoon granulated garlic

¼ teaspoon salt

½ teaspoon freshly ground black pepper

⅓ cup fig jam or preserves

6 slices of bacon, cooked until crispy,
cooled and crumbled

chives or scallions, finely minced, if desired

Lemon Dill Tzatziki

The first time my teenage twins were introduced to Tzatziki, they were hooked. This led to developing a recipe that I could prepare and deliver in containers for late night college study snacks with their dorm friends. You'll find Greek classics developed throughout this cookbook, simply from a love of international fare, that can easily be prepared at home.

About 6 servings

To prepare the cucumber, toss with salt until coated and set in a small colander lined with paper towels to sweat and drain, about 20 minutes. Press the cucumber lightly into the paper towels over a sink, removing any excess liquid. Discard the paper towels and set the cucumbers aside.

In a large bowl, combine the yogurt, sour cream, garlic, dill, olive oil, lemon juice, black pepper and additional salt, if desired. Stir in diced cucumber. Chill for at least one hour, or up to 24 hours. Taste and adjust seasoning before serving. Stays fresh refrigerated in a tightly sealed container up to 3 days. Serve as a dip with vegetables, crackers and/or pita chips.

INGREDIENTS:

½ medium English cucumber, seeded and diced

1½ teaspoons salt, divided, plus more to taste

1 17.6-ounce container 5% whole milk Greek yogurt (2 cups)

¼ cup sour cream

3 cloves garlic, peeled, finely minced

¼ cup chopped fresh dill

1 tablespoon extra virgin olive oil

1 tablespoon freshly squeezed lemon juice

½ teaspoon freshly ground black pepper

sliced cucumbers, bell peppers, grape tomatoes, crackers and/or pita chips, for serving

Slow-Roasted Tomato and Goat Cheese Crostini

Make no mistake, this recipe is a show stopper. The rich and deepened flavor of the slow-roasted tomatoes soaks in like butter on the baguette, enhanced by salty smooth goat cheese, a true winner of an appetizer. Be sure and save the leftover cooking oil, it is a delicious accompaniment for other recipes!

Makes 8 servings

INGREDIENTS:

1 cup extra virgin olive oil, divided

2 pounds fresh plum tomatoes, halved lengthwise, seeded

1 teaspoon dried oregano

1 teaspoon granulated sugar

1 teaspoon salt

2 garlic cloves, peeled and minced

1 tablespoon fresh parsley, finely chopped

6 ounces fresh goat cheese

1 French baguette, cut diagonally into 16 - ½" thick slices, lightly toasted

red onion, finely slivered, for serving, if desired

Preheat oven to 250° F. Coat the bottom of a 9x13" glass baking dish with 2 tablespoons olive oil. Arrange tomatoes in baking dish, cut side up in a single layer. Drizzle remaining olive oil over the tomatoes, and sprinkle evenly with oregano, sugar and salt. Bake for 1 hour. Remove from oven, carefully turn tomatoes over, placing them back in the oil, and return to oven to bake for 1 more hour. Remove from oven, turn the tomatoes cut side up again, bake for 30 minutes more. Remove baking dish from oven, cool slightly.

Using a slotted spoon, place drained tomatoes into a medium bowl or serving dish, reserving oil. Sprinkle garlic and parsley evenly over the tomatoes and between layers. Drizzle tomatoes with half of the cooked oil for serving, and reserve remaining cooked oil for another use (excellent for flavoring Italian dishes). Serve on baguette slices spread with goat cheese, topped with slivered red onions, if desired. Tomatoes keep fresh when refrigerated in a tightly-sealed container up to 4 days, reheat slightly before serving.

Cranberry Rangoon

It was my pleasure to create a recipe series for the Cape Cod Cranberry Growers' Association in 2019. As a New England cook, no cookbook I author could be complete without a collection scattered with cranberry-centered recipes. This was a favorite recipe of the series, offering the sweet and spicy lover's palate a unique go-to for incorporating the fresh berry during its quintessential fall harvest season, as Massachusetts official state fruit. Cranberries also freeze well, and are a great ingredient option for this appetizer.

Makes 16 to 20 rangoon

In a blender, or in the bowl of a food processor, combine cranberries, jalapeño, sugar and mayonnaise, process until smooth. Remove half of mixture to a small bowl, reserving for a dipping sauce. Refrigerate reserved mixture until serving.

Add the softened cream cheese, salt and pepper to the remaining cranberry mixture, process until smooth.

Preheat oven or an air fryer to 400° F. On a clean cutting board, lay out 4 wonton wrappers. Spoon 1 teaspoon of the cream cheese mixture onto the center of each wrapper. Brush 2 adjacent edges of the wrapper with water, folding over the filling in half to form a triangle. Press edges to seal. Place wontons on a greased or parchment-lined baking sheet. Repeat with remaining wrappers and filling.

Bake for 18-20 minutes, or in an air fryer for 8 minutes, moving from top to bottom rack as needed until evenly brown. Serve warm with dipping sauce on the side.

INGREDIENTS:

¾ cup fresh or frozen cranberries, thawed

1 fresh jalapeño pepper, seeded and minced

¼ cup granulated sugar

¼ cup mayonnaise

10 ounces cream cheese, softened

salt and pepper to taste

1 12-ounce package wonton wrappers

1 tablespoon vegetable or canola oil

Garlic Dill Refrigerator Pickles

These pickles make their celebrity appearance at every warm weather party, front and center, whether on a barbeque cookout buffet table or as a cocktail hour appetizer at sunset. Among our friends and family, they have become synonymous with all things summer, and are a frequent gift to fans of all ages. The availability of fresh English cucumbers year round make them an easy refrigerator staple.

Makes 48 spears, or 2 - 32-ounce (1-quart) jars

Prepare the cucumbers: On a large cutting board, cut the cucumbers into 6" segments (or sized for the height of your jars), discarding the trimmed ends. Cut each segment into 6 wedge-shaped spears.

Prepare the brine: Combine the vinegar, salt and sugar in a medium non-reactive saucepan. Cook over medium-high heat, whisking until the salt and sugar are dissolved. Remove from heat, add the ice cubes to the pan, stirring until dissolved.

In 2 - 32-ounce (1-quart) glass jars with tight fitting lids, loosely pack the cucumber spears. Gently insert the fresh dill sprigs and garlic cloves between the cucumbers. In a small bowl, combine the coriander seeds, mustard seeds, red pepper and peppercorns. Divide the spices evenly between the jars. Pour chilled brine evenly into jars, topping off with cold water if needed, until the brine submerges the cucumbers. Cover and refrigerate for 24 hours before serving. After three days, remove the garlic cloves and dill sprigs to preserve flavor and freshness. Pickles stay fresh when refrigerated for up to one week.

INGREDIENTS:

4 English cucumbers (about 2 pounds), rinsed

1¼ cups white vinegar

3 tablespoons coarse salt

2 tablespoons sugar

2 heaping cups ice cubes

8 sprigs fresh dill, stems intact

2 large garlic cloves, peeled and halved

2 tablespoons coriander seeds

1 teaspoon mustard seeds

¼ teaspoon red pepper flakes

2 teaspoons whole black peppercorns

Ultimate Guacamole

Our most requested party recipe of all, Ultimate Guacamole is a kaleidoscope of color and Mexican flavors, easily made in small or party-sized batches.

Makes 12 servings

In a medium bowl, combine avocado and the squeezed juice of one lime. Mash with a fork or masher to desired chunky or smooth consistency. Stir in remaining ingredients, adjusting hot sauce, salt and pepper to desired taste. Cover with plastic wrap, pressing into the guacamole to prevent browning, and refrigerate for 1 hour, or up to 8 hours. Serve with wedges of remaining lime and tortilla chips or sliced vegetables for dipping. Stays fresh when refrigerated in a tightly sealed container up to 3 days, mix leftover guacamole thoroughly before serving.

INGREDIENTS:

3 ripe avocados, pit removed and cubed

2 limes, divided

½ cup grape tomatoes, quartered

¼ cup red onion, finely minced

2 small jalapeño peppers (or ¼ cup pickled jalapeño slices), seeds removed, finely minced

½ teaspoon granulated garlic or garlic powder

⅓ cup sour cream

A few dashes hot sauce

salt and pepper, to taste

1 ear fresh corn, shucked, blanched, kernels stripped

Tortilla chips or sliced vegetables (fresh cucumber, bell pepper or zucchini slices) for serving

Salads

Herbed Lime Garlic Vinaigrette

Greek Salad and Vinaigrette

Though Greek salad is traditionally made with iceberg lettuce, I prefer the crunch or color of spring mix or romaine. To make this favorite dish a dinner salad, add boiled eggs or marinated Greek Grilled Chicken (page 62) after plating. Half of the prepared vinaigrette is used in the salad, the leftovers are great used another day or as a meat marinade.

Makes 4 main course servings of salad
and 8 servings of vinaigrette

Prepare the vinaigrette: In a blender, or a medium bowl, blend or whisk all dressing ingredients until thoroughly combined. Pour into an airtight bottle and store at room temperature up to 8 hours, or until serving. For the remaining leftover dressing, refrigerate until needed, warming to room temperature before use. Keeps fresh when refrigerated up to 2 weeks.

Prepare the salad: In a large salad bowl, layer the salad ingredients, starting with the lettuce as the bottom layer, adding each ingredient in the order they are listed, topping with the olives, feta and pepperoncini. Cover and chill up to 4 hours. To serve, toss with about half of the vinaigrette just prior to plating.

INGREDIENTS:

For the salad:

8-ounces mixed baby lettuces
(red, green or spring mix),
or 1 head of romaine lettuce, chopped

½ English cucumber, coarsely chopped

½ orange bell pepper, core removed,
sliced into ¼" rings

½ medium red onion, sliced into ⅛" rings

1 cup red and/or yellow grape tomatoes

½ cup pitted Kalamata olives

4-ounce block feta cheese, crumbled

¼ cup pickled pepperoncini, sliced

For the vinaigrette:

1 clove of garlic, skin removed, finely minced

1 cup extra virgin olive oil

¼ cup red wine vinegar

2 tablespoons freshly squeezed lemon juice,
from 1 lemon

1 tablespoon grainy brown
or horseradish mustard

1 tablespoon fresh oregano leaves, finely
chopped, or 1 teaspoon dried oregano

1 teaspoon dried thyme

1 teaspoon dried dill weed

2 teaspoons granulated sugar

1 teaspoon salt

½ teaspoon freshly ground black pepper

Herbed Lime Garlic Vinaigrette

Makes about 12 servings

In a medium bowl, combine vinegar, mustard, Worcestershire sauce, lime juice, honey and hot sauce; whisk lightly until thoroughly combined. Slowly drizzle olive oil into mixture, whisking until the dressing emulsifies and slightly thickens. Stir in garlic, herbs, salt and pepper to taste. Serve over tossed salad or use as a meat marinade at room temperature. Keeps fresh when refrigerated in a tightly sealed container up to 1 week. If refrigerated, bring the dressing to room temperature and shake vigorously before serving.

INGREDIENTS:

⅓ cup natural apple cider vinegar
(Bragg's or similar brand)

1½ tablespoons spicy brown
or horseradish brown mustard

2 teaspoons Worcestershire sauce

1 tablespoon fresh squeezed lime juice
from ½ lime

1 tablespoon honey

1 dash hot sauce

⅔ cup extra virgin olive oil

1 large garlic clove, peeled, finely minced

2 tablespoons assorted finely chopped herbs
(dill, parsley and basil)

Salt and freshly ground black pepper to taste

Parmesan Pasta Salad

There are a million pasta salads out there, but this is the one our friends and family decided is our best version, often made with gemelli or shell shaped pasta. A great dish to take to a potluck or make ahead for a speedy weeknight dinner.

Makes 6 servings

In a large bowl, combine pasta, celery, orange pepper, olives, red onion and cucumber. In a medium bowl, whisk together mayonnaise, vinegar, parsley, basil, cheese, poppy seeds, salt and pepper until thoroughly combined. Taste dressing, adjust seasoning to taste. Pour dressing over the pasta and vegetables, tossing to evenly coat. Cover and refrigerate 2 hours or up to 24 hours, serve chilled. Keeps fresh when refrigerated in a tightly sealed container up to 2 days.

INGREDIENTS:

1 pound small shaped pasta, cooked al dente to package directions, drained

¾ cup celery, diced

½ medium orange pepper, cut in 1" strips

½ cup pitted black olives, sliced

½ cup red onion, finely minced

½ cup English cucumber, diced

1¼ cups mayonnaise

2 tablespoons red wine vinegar

2 tablespoons fresh parsley, finely chopped, or 1 tablespoon dried parsley

2 tablespoons fresh basil, finely chopped, or 1 tablespoon dried basil

½ cup parmesan cheese, grated

2 teaspoons poppy seeds

1 teaspoon salt

1 teaspoon freshly ground black pepper

Cranberry Apple Salad

Fruit is a nice addition to a salad, and this recipe is versatile enough to make for just a few or triple to serve a crowd. Consider adding Grilled Greek Chicken (page 62) for a tasty protein on top.

Makes 4 main course servings, or 6-8 side dish salads

Prepare the dressing: In a medium bowl, whisk together lime juice, honey, mustard and spices. Whisk in oil in a thin stream until it emulsifies. Stir in apples. Cover and refrigerate up to 3 hours.

Prepare the salad: In a small bowl, sprinkle sugar over cranberries, toss to coat.

Place lettuce in a large bowl. Pour sugared cranberries and apple mixture over lettuce, toss to evenly coat. Top with scallions and nuts, if desired, and serve immediately.

INGREDIENTS:

Dressing:

2 tablespoons fresh lime juice, squeezed from 1 lime

1 tablespoon honey

1 tablespoon dijon mustard

½ teaspoon celery salt

½ teaspoon onion powder

½ teaspoon dried dill weed

½ teaspoon salt

½ teaspoon freshly ground black pepper

½ cup Extra Virgin Olive Oil

Salad:

1 cup sweetened dried cranberries

1 tablespoon granulated sugar

2 large apples (Cortland or Granny Smith), core removed, cubed

1 large head romaine lettuce, core removed, coarsely chopped or 8-ounces mixed baby red and green leaf lettuce

½ cup scallions, sliced

¾ cup walnuts or pecans, coarsely chopped (optional)

Family Favorite Potato Salad

Our family's potato salad was always my maternal grandmother's original party dish, the recipe has been passed down through the generations. My adaptation incorporates a few alterations that I've learned from other cooks. Alternately, the dish can be transformed by the addition of a tablespoon of dijon mustard, or a few chopped hard boiled eggs folded into the dish before serving.

Makes 8 servings

In a 6-quart pot or Dutch oven, bring 4 quarts water and ½ teaspoon salt to a boil over medium-high heat. Add the cubed potatoes, and boil until just tender when pierced with a fork, about 8-10 minutes. Pour into a colander and drain thoroughly over a sink. Place potatoes in a large serving bowl. Drizzle with vinegar, set aside to completely cool.

In a medium bowl, whisk together mayonnaise, dill, parsley, remaining salt and pepper. Pour the mixture over the potatoes, tossing to coat thoroughly. Taste and adjust seasoning as desired. Cover tightly and refrigerate for at least 2 hours, or up to 24 hours in advance. Garnish with a stem or two of fresh parsley, either whole or chopped, and serve chilled. Stays fresh for up to two days when refrigerated.

INGREDIENTS:

2 teaspoons salt, divided

3 pounds (about 8) white or Yukon Gold potatoes, peeled and cut into ½" cubes

2 tablespoons tarragon, rice or white vinegar

1½ cups mayonnaise

2 medium celery stalks, diced

½ cup sweet onion, diced

1 tablespoon fresh dill, finely chopped

2 tablespoons fresh parsley, finely chopped

1 teaspoon freshly ground black pepper

fresh parsley, for garnish

Shrimp and Apple Salad

This surprising combination of shrimp and apple make for a tasty salad, equally enjoyed served over Boston lettuce leaves or as sandwiches in finger rolls, a favorite for gatherings.

Makes 8-10 servings

INGREDIENTS:

2½ teaspoons salt, divided

2 garlic cloves, peeled, halved

1 lemon, halved

1 bunch fresh dill, divided

1 tablespoon whole peppercorns

2 pounds 21/25 count shrimp, peeled, deveined, tail removed

½ medium red onion, finely chopped

2 stalks of celery, coarsely diced

2 red apples, diced
(Cortland or Fuji varieties are best)

½ cup coarsely chopped walnuts (optional)

1 tablespoon freshly squeezed lemon juice

1 tablespoon red wine or apple cider vinegar

1 teaspoon onion powder or granulated onion

2 teaspoons honey

2 tablespoons horseradish mustard

few dashes of hot sauce

freshly ground black pepper, to taste

⅔ cup mayonnaise

2 heads Boston lettuce, or 10 finger rolls, for serving

Prepare the shrimp: Bring a large pot of water to boil over high heat. Add 2 teaspoons salt, garlic, lemon, 2 stems of fresh dill and peppercorns, stir to combine. Stir in shrimp, return to a simmer, cooking until they are barely opaque and cooked through, about 4 minutes. Carefully pour the pot's contents into a colander, draining water. Discard aromatics, and rinse with cold water to stop the cooking process until cool to the touch. Cut each cooked shrimp into 4 bite-sized pieces, set aside.

Prepare the dressing: Meanwhile, finely chop enough remaining dill, discarding stems, to yield about ⅓ cup. In a small bowl, whisk together lemon juice, vinegar, onion powder, honey, mustard, hot sauce, salt and pepper to taste. Whisk in mayonnaise and chopped dill until smooth.

Assemble the salad: In a large bowl, combine shrimp, red onion, celery, apples and walnuts, if desired. Pour the dressing over the shrimp mixture, and toss lightly until thoroughly combined. Cover and refrigerate until chilled, about 1 hour. Serve over Boston lettuce leaves or in top-sliced finger rolls. Keeps fresh up to 3 days when refrigerated in a tightly sealed container.

Soups

Superfood Chicken Vegetable "Stoup"

Tomato Basil Soup

The use of canned tomatoes makes this soup super convenient year round, when fresh tomatoes are not available. Fresh basil chiffonade and a splash more of cream make a colorful garnish. This is the perfect opportunity to cook up your favorite grilled cheese sandwich to serve on the side, or chop one into ½" cubes as a crouton embellishment.

Makes 6 servings

In a 6-quart non-reactive pot or Dutch oven, melt butter over medium heat. Add onion and carrot and cook until softened, about 4 minutes. Add flour and cook for 1-2 minutes, stirring constantly, taking care not to brown the mixture. Add wine and bring to a simmer for 1 minute. Add tomatoes with juice, broth, tomato paste, basil, thyme and bay leaf. Bring to a simmer, and reduce heat to low. Cover and cook over medium-low heat for 15-20 minutes. Remove from heat and discard the bay leaf. Cool to room temperature.

With an immersion blender or blender, puree soup in batches until smooth. Return to the pan, add cream, heat to a simmer over low heat, about 3 minutes, and adjust seasoning with salt and pepper. Serve hot in bowls garnished with fresh sliced basil and a splash of cream, if desired. Stays fresh when refrigerated up to 3 days in a tightly sealed container.

INGREDIENTS:

2 tablespoons butter

1 medium onion, chopped

1 medium carrot, peeled and diced

2 tablespoons all-purpose unbleached flour

½ cup dry white wine

1 28-ounce can whole plum, diced or crushed tomatoes, juices reserved

1 14.5-ounce can chicken broth

3 tablespoons tomato paste

⅓ cup fresh basil, chopped or 2 tablespoons dried basil

2 teaspoons fresh thyme, or 1 teaspoon dried thyme

1 dried bay leaf

salt and pepper, to taste

1 cup light cream, plus 1 additional tablespoon, for garnish

Fresh basil, finely sliced, for garnish

21

Portuguese Kale Soup

Many New England towns are home to residents of Portuguese descent, the cultural recipes of their origins enjoyably permeate restaurant menus throughout the region. This version was hand scratched on paper among my grandmother's treasures, and over the years, has been adapted to suit the taste of those gathered around our table.

Makes 10 servings

In a large stock pot, sauté diced carrots and onion in vegetable oil over medium heat until tender, about 5 minutes. Stir in chouriço, linguiça or chorizo until color begins to render into the vegetables. Stir in kale and sauté until wilted, about 3 minutes. Add wine, bring to a simmer over medium heat. Add the water and chicken stock, return to a simmer. Reduce heat to medium-low, and stir in tomatoes with liquid, beans, potatoes and vinegar. Simmer for about 40 minutes. Serve steaming in bowls garnished with parmesan cheese.

This soup stays fresh when refrigerated in a tightly sealed container for up to 5 days, or can be frozen for up to 1 month.

Note: *Chouriço (sometimes called linguiça), and chorizo are all good choices for the spicy sausage named as an ingredient in this recipe. Chouriço or linguiça are Portuguese in origins, while chorizo is of Spanish descent. Both sausages are made of pork shoulder, paprika, garlic, black pepper, and salt, with chorizo sporting the highest quantity of paprika. Chouriço or linguiça, have considerably less paprika and a higher ratio of garlic, black pepper as well as Portuguese red wine. The three options are listed to ensure that you'll find one of them local in the region where you reside.*

INGREDIENTS:

2 medium carrots, diced

1 large yellow or white onion, diced

1 tablespoon vegetable oil

1 pound *chouriço, linguiça, or chorizo, cut into ½" dice

1 pound fresh kale, rough stems removed, roughly chopped

½ cup dry white wine

10 cups water

4 cups chicken stock

1 14½-ounce can petite diced tomatoes, liquid reserved

1 15½-ounce can small white or pink beans, drained and rinsed

2 cups red or yellow potatoes, cut into ½" dice

1 tablespoon red wine vinegar

salt and pepper to taste

parmesan cheese, for serving

New England Clam Chowder

The celebration of my Dad's 60th birthday inspired me to adapt favorite versions of this beloved chowder of the northeast for a party for 50 family and friends during a blizzard! The beauty of representing the recipe as a small batch means it can be doubled or tripled to serve a crowd. A warm crock pot set aside mugs and soup spoons with traditional saltine or oyster crackers allow for a self-serve starter while guests mingle. Simmering a batch on the stove top for a few loved ones gathered around your table is just as delightful.

Makes 4 - 2 cup main course servings

In a 6-quart pot or dutch oven, sauté the salt pork over medium-high heat, turning to brown on both sides. Transfer the pork to a paper towel-lined plate to drain. Carefully remove the fat in the pan, reserving about 3 tablespoons of fat. Cool and discard the remainder, or save for another use.

To the same pot, add the onion, celery and carrot to the fat and sauté over medium-low heat until softened. Stir in the potatoes, spices and water, cover and simmer for 10 minutes. Uncover and cook 12 more minutes, until most of the liquid has evaporated.

Meanwhile, pour the half and half into a medium saucepan, and heat gently over medium-low heat until barely simmering at the edges, stirring frequently to prevent scorching. Dice cooked salt pork into small cubes, set aside.

Stir clams and the clam juice or liquor into the potato mixture, and simmer for 2 minutes, barely cooking the clams through (overcooking the clams will result in a rubbery texture). Stir in the half and half, parmesan cheese and salt pork. Cook 1 more minute to thoroughly incorporate and heat through, remove from heat. Taste to adjust seasoning, and serve hot topped with chives, if desired. Chowder stays fresh up to 3 days when refrigerated in a tightly-sealed container, reheat to serve.

INGREDIENTS:

6 ounces salt pork, rind discarded, rinsed and cut into ¼" strips

2 medium onions, peeled, diced

1 large celery stalk, coarsely chopped

1 small carrot, peeled, finely chopped

4 small red potatoes, diced in ½" cubes

2 teaspoons dried dill

1 teaspoon dried thyme

1½ teaspoons salt

1 teaspoon freshly ground pepper

2 cups water

50 medium hard shell clams, shucked, chopped, clam liquor reserved

- or -

2 6½-ounce cans chopped clams, drained, plus 16-ounces bottled clam juice

3 cups half and half

½ cup grated parmesan cheese

Fresh chives, finely chopped, for serving if desired

Sherried Mushroom Bisque

Mushrooms are the star of many of my recipes, because they are one of my favorite vegetables. Each time I prepare this bisque, those enjoying it with me at the table are always comforted by the rich goodness that wafts from the earthy ingredients and the sweet note of sherry in the air.

Makes 6 servings

In a 6-quart pot or dutch oven, melt the butter over low heat. Stir in the green onions and thyme, and simmer over low heat for 10 minutes, taking care not to brown or burn the mixture. Stir in flour to create a roux, and cook for 1-2 minutes. Pour in stock, wine, mushrooms, salt and pepper, and return to a simmer, cooking uncovered for 15 minutes. Remove from the heat and cool to room temperature.

Using a blender or immersion blender, carefully process the bisque until smooth, in batches if necessary. Return to the pot, and stir in the cream and sherry. Reheat until barely simmering and heated through. Taste and adjust seasoning, and serve hot. *Stays fresh when refrigerated in a tightly sealed container up to 4 days.

*Note: *I love to make soups in large batches and freeze them in individual serving containers to reheat for a warm lunch in winter. If you wish to freeze this bisque, omit the cream during preparation and add upon reheating before serving.*

INGREDIENTS:

6 tablespoons butter

1 teaspoon dried thyme leaves

1 bunch scallions, white and green parts thinly sliced

3 tablespoons all-purpose unbleached flour

4 cups chicken stock

½ cup dry white wine

2 12-ounce packages fresh white mushrooms, quartered

1 teaspoon salt

1 teaspoon freshly ground black pepper

1 cup heavy cream

⅓ cup dry sherry

Curried Butternut Apple Bisque

Once winter squash comes into season, this is a great way to bring the scent of roasting goodness to your kitchen, and warmth to the bowls on your table. Add the cream if you're looking for a rich bisque, but taste it first, as the depth of flavor often stands on its own without the dairy addition.

Makes 12 servings

INGREDIENTS:

2 medium butternut squash, halved and seeded

5 tablespoons butter, divided

1 large onion, chopped

2 large apples, peeled and cubed

12 dried cherries
or 18 sweetened dried cranberries

2 teaspoons ground ginger

1 teaspoon ground sage

1½ teaspoons yellow curry powder

2 teaspoons salt

1 teaspoon freshly ground black pepper

½ cup apple cider

1 cup dry white wine

2 cups vegetable stock

1 cup light cream, optional

Preheat oven to 400° F. Brush cut side of squash with 1 tablespoon of melted butter, place cut side down on a greased baking sheet. Roast for 45-60 minutes, until fork tender. Remove from oven, and set aside to cool to room temperature. In a large bowl, scoop out the flesh, discarding the skin, set aside.

In a 6-quart pot or Dutch oven, sauté the remaining butter and onion until soft. Add squash, apples, cherries or cranberries, spices, cider, wine and vegetable stock. Cover and simmer for 25 minutes over medium-low heat. Remove from heat, cool slightly and process soup in batches in a blender, food processor, or with an immersion blender until smooth. Return to pot, and add cream, if desired. Bring back to temperature over medium-low heat, adjusting seasoning to taste, and serve hot. Keeps fresh when refrigerated in a tightly sealed container for up to 4 days. Freezes well, when stored without the addition of the cream, up to one month.

Lemony Asparagus Mushroom Soup with Chicken

INGREDIENTS:

3 slices bacon

1 tablespoon butter or oil

1 12-ounce package fresh button mushrooms, cleaned and sliced, divided

1 cup celery, diced

1 Vidalia or sweet onion, roughly chopped

1 pound fresh asparagus, woody portion discarded, chopped in 1" segments

1 large clove garlic, peeled, finely chopped

1 full bunch parsley, stems removed, finely chopped, divided

¼ cup fresh thyme, finely chopped

¼ cup fresh basil, finely chopped

salt and pepper to taste

1 cup dry white wine or water

2 cooked chicken breasts (pre-cooked or rotisserie), chopped

1 32-ounce container chicken or vegetable stock

1 32-ounce container chicken or vegetable broth

arrowroot powder, as needed

1 fresh lemon, rind grated and reserved, juice squeezed and reserved

½ cup heavy cream

Delicious and different! Be sure to use HEAVY cream because the lemon juice will curdle any other type of milk. I often opt to use the breasts of a rotisserie chicken to simplify the process. Arrowroot powder is a great thickening agent, as well all-natural and gluten-free, and requires no cold water or roux incorporation like cornstarch or flour, which can be substituted.

Makes 14 servings

In a 6-quart pot or dutch oven, cook bacon until the fat is rendered and the meat is crispy. Remove the bacon with a slotted spoon to a paper towel lined plate and cool. Crumble and set aside. In the same pot, add butter or oil. Sauté ⅔ of the sliced mushrooms until brown, reserving the rest. Remove from pan and set aside to cool.

To the same pan, add reserved mushrooms, celery, onion, asparagus, garlic, half of parsley, thyme, basil, salt and pepper to taste, and sauté over medium heat until tender, about 5 minutes. Add wine or water, cook 2 minutes. Add chicken or vegetable broth and stock, cover, simmer over low heat for 15-20 minutes, remove from heat and cool to room temperature.

Carefully process the soup, in batches if necessary, in a blender or with an immersion blender until smooth. Return to stove top over medium heat, simmer for 2 minutes. Stir in 1 tablespoon arrowroot powder, whisking to blend. Bring the soup back to a simmer. Adjust arrowroot addition to achieve desired thickness. Pour in lemon juice and heavy cream. Add in sautéed mushrooms, remaining parsley, lemon rind, and chopped bacon. Serve hot in bowls. Stays fresh when refrigerated in a tightly sealed container up to 4 days.

Superfood Chicken Vegetable "Stoup"

This soup/stew was "imagineered" in my kitchen as a tribute to all the soup fans out there! I focused on including high-nutrition veggies, with plenty of superfoods like parsley, spinach and cabbage, and a little chicken as protein for balance. This would be an excellent soup to make for a sick friend, or to freeze for reheating on a snowy afternoon for lunch.

Makes 16 - 1½ cup servings

Prepare the stock: Season the chicken thighs with 1 teaspoon salt and ground black pepper. Heat a large stock pot or Dutch oven over medium-high heat, place the chicken thighs, coated in vegetable oil, skin side down. Sear the chicken until the skin is golden brown, then flip thighs skin side up, reducing temperature to prevent smoking. Surround the thighs with carrots, celery, onion, scallions, garlic, spices, remaining salt and peppercorns, stirring frequently, and sauté until they are fragrant and become slightly tender, about 6 minutes. Stir in lemon, ⅓ bunch parsley and water, cover and bring to a simmer. Continue cooking for 20 minutes. Remove from heat, cool to room temperature.

Strain the stock by pouring through a colander into a large pot or bowl, reserving the liquid and chicken, discarding the chicken skin, lemon, aromatics and vegetables. On a cutting board, separate the chicken from the bones, discarding the skin, bones and cartilage. Coarsely chop the remaining chicken, cover the stock and chicken, reserving for stoup.

Prepare the stoup: In the same stock pot or Dutch oven, sauté carrots, celery, onions, spices, salt and pepper in oil or bacon fat until softened and fragrant, about 4 minutes. Add the wine, if desired, and cook for 2 minutes more. Pour in the strained chicken stock, cabbage, peas, mushrooms, tomatoes, spinach and cauliflower rice. Cover and simmer over medium low heat for 20 minutes, or until the vegetables are tender. Stir in the chopped cooked chicken, simmer for 5 minutes more and serve hot. Keeps fresh when refrigerated in a tightly sealed container up to 3 days, or frozen up to one month.

INGREDIENTS:

Chicken Stock:

1½ pounds bone-in chicken thighs, skin intact

1 tablespoon salt, divided

½ teaspoon freshly ground black pepper

1 tablespoon vegetable oil

1 carrot, cut in 2" sections

2 celery stalks, cut in 2" sections

1 small onion, peeled and quartered

6 scallions, cut in 2" sections

½ head garlic, cut in half crosswise, skin and stem end intact

½ teaspoon red pepper flakes

2 teaspoons dried basil

1 teaspoon dried thyme

1 tablespoon salt

2 teaspoons whole black peppercorns

½ lemon, sliced

⅓ bunch fresh parsley, stems intact, remainder reserved for stoup

8 cups water

Stoup:

1 tablespoon bacon fat or vegetable oil

2-3 large carrots, diced

½ bunch celery stalks, diced

1 large or 2 small onions, diced

2 teaspoons dried basil

1 teaspoon dried thyme

⅔ bunch fresh parsley, stems removed, finely chopped (reserved from stock)

1 teaspoon salt

½ teaspoon freshly ground black pepper

½ cup dry white wine, optional

8 cups chicken stock

½ medium green cabbage, core removed, finely sliced

1 12-ounce package fresh or frozen peas

1 12-ounce package fresh mushrooms, sliced

1 14.5 ounce can petite diced tomatoes, juice reserved

1 16-ounce container fresh baby spinach, coarsely chopped

10-12 ounces fresh cauliflower rice

Chopped cooked chicken thighs, reserved from stock

Potsticker Soup

I'll admit it, I love soup, as you'll likely be aware by the number of soup recipes in this book. My children hadn't developed the same affection during their grade school years, so I crafted this satisfying soup recipe to keep us all happy. After all, most children will do just about anything to eat a potsticker.

Makes 4 main-course servings

In a medium skillet, sauté frozen potstickers in 1 tablespoon oil over medium heat, turning to brown on two sides, about 6 minutes. Pour water into the pan, and cover immediately with a lid. Reduce heat to medium low, and simmer for 3-4 minutes until the water has evaporated, and the potstickers are cooked through. Set aside.

In a 6-8 quart pot, sauté cabbage, mushrooms, carrots and celery in 1 tablespoon oil over medium-high heat for 2 minutes, stirring constantly. Add peas and white parts of the sliced scallions, cook 2 minutes. Stir in broth, sesame oil, soy sauce or Tamari, salt and pepper and simmer until the vegetables are tender, about 10 minutes.

To serve, divide the potstickers evenly among 4 soup bowls. Ladle soup over potstickers, garnish with sliced green scallions. Store leftover soup and potstickers separately in tightly sealed containers. Keeps fresh up to 4 days when refrigerated. Reheat leftover soup and potstickers separately, then combine to serve.

INGREDIENTS:

1 16-ounce package (20-24) frozen potstickers

2 tablespoons vegetable oil, divided

2 tablespoons water

3 cups napa cabbage, thinly sliced

1 12-ounce package button mushrooms, thinly sliced

2 carrots, finely chopped

2 stalks celery, thinly sliced

1 cup frozen or fresh peas

1 cup fresh scallions, white and green parts divided, sliced

6 cups chicken broth, store bought or homemade

1 teaspoon sesame oil

few dashes soy sauce or Tamari sauce

½ teaspoon salt

½ teaspoon freshly ground black pepper

Sides

Classic Coleslaw

Almond Apple Rice

This is a lovely combination of salty and sweet flavors, and the juice really raises simple white rice to a new taste level.

Makes 4-6 servings

In a medium saucepan, bring apple juice or cider and water, 1 tablespoon butter and salt to a boil. Stir in rice and cover. Reduce heat to low, and simmer for 20-25 minutes, or until the liquid is absorbed. Remove from heat, and rest, covered, for 5 minutes. Fluff with a fork.

Meanwhile, sauté almonds in remaining butter until lightly browned, stirring constantly, taking care not to burn. Fold the almonds into the rice, along with fresh parsley, if desired. Serve hot. Can be made early in day and reheated to serve.

INGREDIENTS:

2 cups apple juice, or 1 cup apple cider mixed with 1 cup water

4 tablespoons butter, divided

1 teaspoon salt

1 cup long-grain white rice

½ cup sliced almonds, ½ cup whole roasted almonds, coarsely chopped

½ teaspoon freshly ground black pepper

¼ cup fresh parsley, chopped (optional)

Mashed Sour Sweet Potatoes

As simple as it gets, but don't overlook the juxtaposition of the potato sweetness with the sour in the cream. It is a winning combo, and easily doubled or tripled to serve a crowd.

Makes 4 servings

Preheat oven to 400° F Pierce the skin of the sweet potatoes with a fork, place in the center rack in the oven and bake until fork tender, about 40-50 minutes. Remove from oven, set aside to cool for 5 minutes. Cut each potato in half. In a medium bowl, squeeze the potato out, discarding the skin. Add the butter, and mash until smooth and most lumps are gone. Stir in sour cream, salt and pepper until thoroughly combined. Serve hot.

INGREDIENTS:

2 large sweet potatoes

1 tablespoon butter

½ cup sour cream

1 teaspoon salt

½ teaspoon freshly-ground pepper

Sautéed Garlic Spinach

Makes 4 servings

In a large skillet, sauté the shallot in butter and olive oil over medium heat until translucent and softened. Top with handfuls of baby spinach, mounding the pan.* Sauté, stirring frequently, turning the spinach until all of it has wilted. Using a flat spatula or wooden spoon, push the spinach aside, and spread the garlic over half the pan. Pull the spinach back over to cover the garlic, and cook untouched for about 3 minutes over medium heat, or until the garlic is light brown and toasted.

Add the wine or water to create steam, stirring the spinach until it reduces and the stems are soft and tender, stirring frequently. Season evenly with salt and pepper, taste to adjust seasoning to taste and serve hot.

***Note:** Fresh spinach reduces drastically when it is cooked. If all of the spinach won't fit in the pan at first, fit what you can, and as it wilts, add more until all the spinach is incorporated.*

INGREDIENTS:

1 tablespoon olive oil

1 tablespoon butter

1 large shallot, finely minced

16 ounces fresh baby spinach

3 cloves garlic, finely minced

2 tablespoons dry white wine or water

1 teaspoon salt

½ teaspoon freshly ground black pepper

Classic Coleslaw

Another adapted version of a family favorite, passed down through a few generations, still making guests smile when served at a summer cookout.

Makes 8 servings

In a large bowl, whisk together mayonnaise, vinegar, honey, sugar and spices until smooth. Set aside.

Cut the cabbage into 8 small wedges, removing core. Using a food processor or mandoline slicer, finely shred cabbage and celery to uniform size thin slices. Using a grater, finely shred the carrot. Add vegetables to the dressing bowl, and toss to coat, combining thoroughly. The slaw will appear dry when first prepared, but will soften and release liquid as it chills, thinning the dressing.

Refrigerate for at least 1 hour, toss before serving. Stays fresh when refrigerated up to 24 hours.

INGREDIENTS:

¾ cup mayonnaise

3 tablespoons apple cider vinegar

2 tablespoons honey

2 teaspoons sugar

1 teaspoon salt

½ teaspoon freshly ground black pepper

1 teaspoon paprika

1 teaspoon celery seed

½ medium head green cabbage

2 medium stalks celery

1 large carrot

Vegetable Tian Gratin

A kaleidoscope of color showcasing summer's bounty, best made when the featured vegetables are in season.

Makes 8 servings

In a medium skillet, heat the garlic and olive oil over medium-low heat. Sauté, stirring constantly until fragrant, about 3 minutes. Remove from heat, stir in 1 tablespoon fresh thyme or 1½ teaspoon dried thyme, 2 tablespoons fresh basil or 1 tablespoon dried basil, 1 teaspoon salt, and ½ teaspoon pepper, and set aside.

Prepare the vegetables: On a mandoline slicer or using a very sharp knife on a cutting board, uniformly slice the vegetables to ⅛" thick, discarding stem ends. Set aside in stacks for assembly.

Preheat oven to 375° F. In a greased 9-inch square baking dish, or one of similar size, layer the vegetables on end, alternating tomatoes, zucchini, summer squash, onions and quartered slices of provolone or American cheese to form sideways stacks, using a pastry brush to lightly apply the seasoned olive oil mixture between each vegetable/cheese addition. Repeat until all the vegetables are assembled. (Tip: for baking dishes that have squared-off sides, you may want to turn the dish on its end while assembling, allowing the stacks to stand upright, and then return the dish to its regular upright position when assembly is complete).

Drizzle the tian with the remaining seasoned olive oil. Top with parmesan cheese, remaining thyme, basil, and salt and pepper, adjusting seasoning to taste. Bake for 50-60 minutes, until bubbling and the top is golden brown. Serve warm.

INGREDIENTS:

6 tablespoons olive oil, divided

3 medium garlic cloves, peeled, finely minced

5 tablespoons fresh thyme leaves,
or 2½ teaspoons dried thyme, divided

⅓ cup fresh basil, finely chopped, divided

1½ teaspoons salt, divided, more to taste

1 teaspoon freshly ground black pepper, divided, more to taste

3 large ripe, firm beefsteak-variety tomatoes, cored

2 medium zucchini

2 medium summer squash

2 medium sweet onions
(Vidalia or Walla Walla), peel removed

¾ pound provolone or American cheese, thinly sliced and quartered

1 teaspoon salt, divided

1¼ cups grated or shredded parmesan cheese

Pork and Beef

Butternut Béchamel Lasagna

Keftedes Burgers

Greek themed recipes continue their appearance throughout this collection, seen here in this delicious and unique burger, served plated with plenty of sides and condiments, meant to be eaten with a fork or slid into a quarter loaf of pita bread just before your first bite.

Makes 4 servings

Prepare the burgers: In a large bowl, combine pork, red onion, parsley, pine nuts, garlic, feta cheese, lemon juice and spices until evenly distributed. Using your hands, form 4 firm patties, and set on a plate. Grill burgers or sear in a cast iron pan over medium-high heat until thoroughly cooked through, and burgers are no longer pink in the center when tested, about 6-8 minutes.

To serve, arrange burgers among piles of arugula or spring mix, tomato, red onion, cucumber, feta cheese and Kalamata olives on a serving plate, or divide evenly for individual servings on 4 dinner plates. Serve with a bowl of Tzatziki sauce on the side and pita wedges.

Note: *The pita bread is equally tasty served at room temperature, or brushed lightly with a mixture of olive oil, a clove of pressed garlic, salt and pepper, and warmed on a hot grill until grill marks appear.*

INGREDIENTS:

For the burgers:

1 pound ground pork

¼ cup red onion, finely chopped

3 tablespoons pine nuts

3 medium cloves garlic, finely minced

½ cup feta cheese, fork crumbled from a brick

1 tablespoon lemon juice, from ½ squeezed fresh lemon

¼ cup fresh parsley, chopped

1 teaspoon onion powder

1 teaspoon dried oregano

½ teaspoon dried thyme

½ teaspoon paprika

½ teaspoon salt

½ teaspoon freshly ground black pepper

For serving:

2 cups fresh arugula or spring mix lettuce, loosely packed

1 beefsteak-variety tomato, sliced

½ red onion, thinly sliced

1 cucumber, diagonally sliced

1 8-ounce jar roasted red peppers, drained and sliced

8-ounces feta cheese, fork crumbled from a brick

oil-marinated Kalamata olives

1 cup Lemon Dill Tzatziki Sauce (see page 6, or use store-bought Tzatziki)

1 package (4 loaves) pita bread, quartered into wedges

*olive oil, 1 clove garlic, salt and pepper to taste, if desired

Celebration Filet Mignon
with Cherry Balsamic Reduction

Filet has long been my favorite cut of beef. An opportunity to enter a romantic menu competition inspired the creation of a reduction sauce as the beef's best complement, resulting in a winning entry, recreated many times since marking life's many celebrations.

Makes 2 servings

Prepare the reduction: In a small saucepan over low heat, sauté 1 tablespoon butter and shallots until translucent and softened, about 3 minutes. Stir in cherries or cranberries and thyme, and sauté for 2 minutes more, until fragrant. Stir in the wine, vinegar and honey, bring to a simmer over medium heat. Simmer uncovered until reduced by half, about 15 minutes. Set aside.

Prepare the steaks: Preheat oven to 400° F. In a small bowl, combine garlic, thyme, salt and pepper. Pat the surfaces of the steaks dry with a paper towel. Sprinkle the herb mixture on both cut sides of the steak evenly, pressing to adhere. Set aside on a covered plate to bring up to room temperature, about 30 minutes.

In a medium cast iron skillet, heat butter over medium-high heat, until butter melts to sizzling. Sear the steaks untouched for 2-3 minutes on each side, until brown. Insert a meat thermometer into one steak, and transfer covered skillet to oven to desired doneness.* Remove from oven, and allow to rest covered for 5-10 minutes, to preserve the juices before serving.

To serve: Reheat the reduction slightly over medium-low heat, stirring in remaining 1 tablespoon butter until melted and incorporated. Strain and discard the solids from the sauce, reserving the liquid into a serving pitcher or side dish bowls. Serve steaks with the warm reduction on the side.

*Notes: *Stove top cooking at high temperature tends to emit smoke. Open a nearby window and turn on your stove's vent fan to aid safe ventilation. If the pan emits excessive smoke from being overheated, remove from heat to cool. Use an oven mitt when handling a cast iron skillet, as the handle often becomes very hot during cooking.*

Bring the temperature of the steak to 5-10 degrees below desired doneness before removing from oven, as the meat will continue to cook as it rests. I recommend cooking filet steak to medium rare to showcase its lean and tender qualities.

Steak cooking temperatures:

Rare:	120° F to 125° F
Medium rare:	125° F to 130° F
Medium:	135° F to 140° F
Medium well:	145° F to 150° F
Well done:	160° F and above

INGREDIENTS:

For the steaks:

2 8-ounce filet mignon steaks, cut 1½-2" thick

½ teaspoon granulated garlic

1 teaspoon dried thyme

1 teaspoon salt

½ teaspoon freshly ground black pepper

¼ cup butter

For the reduction:

2 tablespoons butter, divided

1 shallot, peeled, finely minced

⅓ cup dried cherries
or sweetened dried cranberries

2 teaspoons dried thyme

¾ cup dry red wine

⅓ cup balsamic vinegar

1 tablespoon honey

Mom's Meatballs

Every family has a go-to recipe, right? This is more of an American-Italian version of the comforting classic, but it sure has satisfied many a plate in our kitchen.

Makes 20-24 - 2" meatballs

Tear bread into small pieces and pulse into crumbs in a food processor or mini-chopper. Soak the bread crumbs in the half and half or milk in a small bowl, set aside.

In a large bowl, combine the beef, pork, parmesan cheese, parsley, basil, onion, garlic, eggs, salt and pepper, mix until thoroughly combined. Form mixture by hand into 2" round meatballs, and set on a lightly greased baking sheet. Refrigerate for 1 hour, or up to 24 hours before baking.

Preheat the oven to 350° F. Brush the chilled meatballs with olive oil, and bake for 20-25 minutes, until lightly browned. Place the meatballs in a pot of your favorite tomato sauce, and simmer lightly until heated back through. Serve with pasta of choice, or toast sliced sub rolls to make meatball subs, adding meatballs and sauce, topped with mozzarella cheese and broiled under low heat until the cheese melts and is bubbling.

INGREDIENTS:

2 slices white or sourdough bread

¼ cup half and half or milk

1 pound 80% lean ground beef

½ pound ground pork

½ cup parmesan cheese, grated or finely shredded

¼ cup fresh Italian parsley, finely chopped

¼ cup fresh basil, finely chopped

½ cup white or yellow onion, very finely chopped

2 large cloves garlic, peeled, finely minced

2 large eggs, beaten

2 teaspoons salt

1 teaspoon freshly ground black pepper

¼ cup olive oil

For serving:

Pasta of choice, or sub rolls

6 cups prepared tomato sauce

Sliced mozzarella or provolone cheese, if desired

Reuben Stacks

When you love reuben sandwiches as much as this family does, you concoct new creations with the same variety of ingredients. The benefit here is that all the deliciousness comes through from the tasty treat without added bread, yielding a much more dinner-worthy plate.

Makes 4 servings

Prepare the sauce: In a small bowl, stir together the dressing and chopped pickle, chill covered until serving, up to two days in advance.

In a 10" cast iron pan or non-stick skillet, heat the butter, oil and garlic until melted and fragrant, about 2 minutes. Place the 4 cabbage wedges cut side down in the pan, searing until the cut edges are golden brown, about 3-4 minutes each cut side. Set cabbage aside.

In the same pan, sauté the onion in the remaining fat over medium heat for about 5 minutes, stirring frequently, until softened and lightly browned. Set onions aside.

Meanwhile, cut the corned beef slices to be uniform in size to that of a medium quartered cabbage leaf. Carefully lift the quartered cabbage leaves, keeping the stem end intact, and insert corned beef slices between, equally for each wedge. Return the stacks to the skillet, add a half cup of water and the spices, cover with a lid. Braise for 10-15 minutes on the stovetop over medium heat, or until the cabbage is tender when tested with a fork. Remove the lid and top each wedge with 2 slices of cheese and the sautéed onions, evenly divided. Replace the lid and cook over low heat for 5 minutes, until the cheese is melted. Serve hot with side bowls of tangy sauce.

INGREDIENTS:

1 medium fresh green cabbage, quartered, stem intact

2 tablespoons butter

1 tablespoon vegetable oil

1 clove garlic, peeled, finely minced

1 medium yellow or sweet onion, sliced into rings

1 pound corned beef (thick deli slices or from a cooked corned beef roast)

8 slices Swiss cheese

1 teaspoon granulated garlic or garlic powder

1 teaspoon dried thyme

½ teaspoon freshly ground black pepper

Tangy sauce:

1 cup thousand island dressing

1 medium dill pickle spear, finely chopped

Asian Beef and Noodles

During a visit with my three adult children, I asked which recipes they'd most want me to include in this cookbook. My son's instantaneous answer was Asian Beef and Noodles, stating "that dish is a staple of my youth!" The reason for his response, I believe, is that it is easily doubled or tripled to satisfy growing appetites, adaptable to preferred vegetables or leftover beef, conveniently paired with pantry-staple ramen or store-bought noodles, and enjoyed by all ages!

Makes 4 servings

Prepare the steak (if not using leftover): Trim fat from steak; cut across grain into ½ x 1" strips. Heat vegetable oil in a large wok or skillet over medium-high heat to sizzling. Add steak and stir fry until cooked through to medium-rare doneness, about 3 minutes. Remove steak from pan, set aside on a plate to rest, keeping warm.

In the same pan, stir fry the green beans, mushrooms, ginger and garlic until tender and softened, about 3 minutes. Remove vegetables from pan, keeping warm.

Prepare the noodles: If not using fresh noodles, remove ramen bricks from packaging; discard seasoning packets. Add broth to the same pan, bring to a simmer over medium heat. Break ramen squares in half, add ramen or fresh noodles to broth. Cook uncovered for 4 minutes over medium-low heat, or until the liquid is absorbed, stirring frequently. Stir in sliced steak, cooked vegetables, scallions, sesame oil, soy sauce or tamari and black pepper to taste, turning to coat until heated through, serve hot. Leftovers keep fresh when refrigerated in a tightly sealed containers for 2 days.

INGREDIENTS:

1 16-ounce ribeye steak (or 16 ounces leftover steak, rare-medium, sliced in ½" strips)

2 teaspoons vegetable oil

12 ounces fresh green beans, stem end removed, cut in half

1 12-ounce package fresh button mushrooms, thinly sliced

1½ tablespoons fresh ginger, finely grated

3 cloves fresh garlic, finely minced

2 2.8-ounce packages ramen noodles (or 3 cups fresh Asian noodles, prepared to directions)

1 14.5 ounce can beef broth

1 cup fresh scallions, thinly sliced

2 teaspoons sesame oil

1 tablespoon soy sauce or tamari sauce

freshly ground black pepper, to taste

Spicy Cheesy Sausage Pasta

Create a few smiles with this sausage and pasta dish featuring colorful vegetables in a spicy basil parmesan sauce. This is a perfect opportunity to refine your al dente pasta cooking skills, as the simmer-in-sauce moment at the end will continue cooking the pasta slightly before serving.

Makes 6 servings

Sauté sausage in a medium skillet coated in 2 teaspoons olive oil until cooked through and golden brown. Cool slightly, slice into ¼" thick coins, cover to keep warm and set aside.

In the same pan, melt butter and remaining olive oil, and sauté bell pepper, shallot, sun-dried tomatoes, garlic and red pepper until softened. Stir in the artichoke hearts and 3 tablespoons basil, heat until warmed through, set aside.

In a 6-quart pot or dutch oven, boil pasta according to package directions in salted water to al dente firmness. Drain in a colander, reserving ½ cup cooking water, set aside.

In the same pot, stir together cooking water and wine until heated through. Stir in heavy cream, ⅔ cup cheese, salt and pepper. Once the cheese melts, remove from heat, and return the pasta to the pot, combining thoroughly with the sauce, stirring to coat. Stir in sausage, and serve topped with remaining parmesan cheese and fresh basil as garnish.

INGREDIENTS:

4 links Asiago garlic (or similar variety) sausage

2 tablespoons Extra Virgin Olive Oil, divided

2 tablespoons butter

1 orange bell pepper, sliced

1 large shallot, coarsely chopped

¼ cup sun-dried tomatoes in olive oil, finely minced

3 large cloves garlic, finely minced

½ teaspoon dried red pepper flakes

1 6-ounce jar/can marinated artichoke heart quarters, liquid reserved, coarsely chopped

¼ cup fresh basil, finely slivered, divided

1 pound dry pasta, vermicelli or other variety

½ cup pasta cooking water

½ cup dry white wine

⅓ cup heavy cream

1 cup parmesan cheese, grated, divided

1 teaspoon salt

1 teaspoon freshly ground pepper

Butternut Béchamel Lasagna with Sage and Sausage

This culinary invention celebrates all things fall in a crowd pleasing dish that is generous in size. It can be halved for a smaller lasagna, or prepared in two pans, to keep one to freeze or gift to a friend.

Makes 10-12 servings

Early in the day, preheat oven to 400° F. Brush cut sides of squash with melted butter. Roast cut side down on a greased baking sheet for 45-60 minutes, until fork tender. Set aside to cool to room temperature. Peel the skin away from the squash, placing the squash into a large mixing bowl, discarding skin and any crusted edges. Mash until smooth, season with salt and pepper, set aside.

Prepare béchamel: Melt butter in a medium saucepan over medium heat. Add minced onion and sauté for 2-3 minutes, until softened and translucent. Add flour, stirring constantly to make a roux. Cook 2 minutes over medium heat, taking care not to burn. Add milk in three stages, constantly stirring until slightly thickened. Stir in sage, nutmeg, sherry or wine, salt and pepper. Stir slowly into mashed squash, folding until evenly combined with a spatula. Set aside, or chill until needed for lasagna assembly.

In a 6-quart pot, boil lasagna noodles according to package directions to al dente consistency in salted water. Carefully pour contents of pot into a colander over a sink, and rinse with cool water to stop the cooking process and prevent noodles from sticking, drain. Lay the noodles flat on a greased baking sheet, spraying between layers with cooking spray, cover with wax paper until assembly.

Assemble lasagna: Preheat the oven to 350° F. Lightly coat lasagna pan with cooking spray. Smear a thin layer of the squash mixture to coat bottom of pan. Create 5 layers of side-by-side lasagna noodles, topping each layer with equal amounts of squash mixture, thinly sliced sausages, and shredded cheese. Repeat until ingredients are consumed, if desired, finishing the top with remaining shredded cheese.

Loosely cover with tin foil and bake for 40 minutes, uncover and bake for 10-20 minutes more, or until mozzarella has melted and just starting to brown. Serve immediately. Keeps fresh when stored in a tightly sealed container and refrigerated up to 3 days. May be frozen up to one month and reheated after thawing to room temperature.

INGREDIENTS:

For squash:

1 large butternut squash, halved and seeded

1 tablespoon butter, melted

salt and pepper, to taste

For bechamel:

6 tablespoons butter

½ onion, finely minced

3 tablespoons all-purpose unbleached flour

2½ cups whole or low-fat milk

8 fresh sage leaves, finely minced

¾ teaspoon nutmeg

2 tablespoons dry sherry or white wine

2 teaspoons salt

1 teaspoon freshly ground black pepper

For lasagna:

16 ounces shredded mozzarella cheese

salt, to taste

1 package traditional lasagna noodles

6-8 cooked sweet Italian sausage,
finely slivered into coins

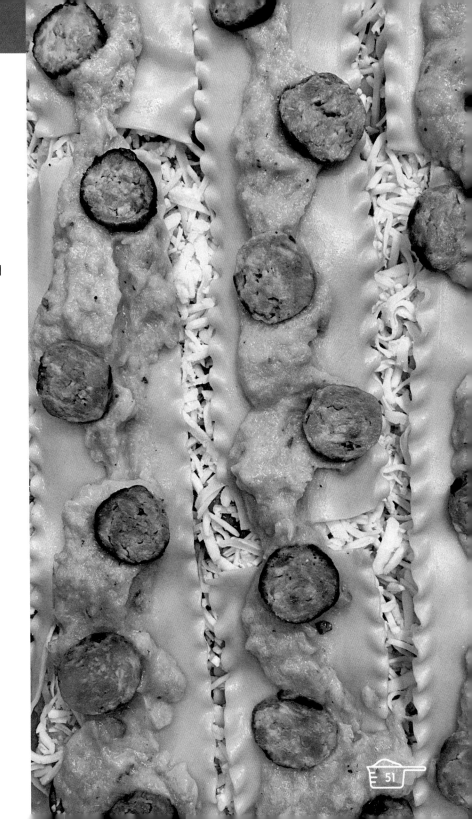

Stuffed Rainbow Peppers

A benefit of caring for my grandmother in our home for a few years was the sharing of recipes from over the course of her 90-year life. This adaptation of an American classic was inspired by her version, carefully penned on a scrap of paper, still in my possession. It has evolved into an elevated main dish favorite for family and friends alike.

Makes 6 servings

In a medium saucepan, combine broth, rice, onion, garlic and mushrooms, if desired. Cover with a tight fitting lid, and simmer over low heat until the liquid is absorbed, about 15-20 minutes. Remove from heat, set aside to cool.

Meanwhile, in a large bowl, combine ground beef, Worcestershire sauce, thyme, black pepper and salt. Using clean hands, knead to combine. Stir in 1 cup tomato sauce and the rice mixture, and knead with clean hands until thoroughly combined.

Preheat oven to 350° F. Place peppers cut side up in a greased 9x13" baking dish or on a greased baking sheet. Fill peppers equally with generous amounts of the meat mixture, pressing firmly to mound and set. Top equally with remaining tomato sauce, followed by the shredded cheese. Cover loosely with tin foil and bake for 45-55 minutes, until the center of the stuffing is cooked through. Remove foil and broil on low for 2-3 minutes to lightly brown the cheese, if desired. Serve topped with pan juices.

INGREDIENTS:

1 14½-ounce can beef broth

¾ cup white long-grain rice

½ cup white or yellow onion, diced

3 garlic cloves, finely minced

8 ounces fresh button mushrooms, finely chopped (optional)

1 pound 85% lean ground beef

2 teaspoons Worcestershire sauce

2 teaspoons fresh thyme leaves or 1 teaspoon dried thyme

1 teaspoon freshly ground black pepper

1 teaspoon salt

1 15-ounce can tomato sauce

3 large yellow, orange or red bell peppers, halved, cored, seeds removed

1 cup shredded cheddar cheese

Poultry

Ginger Amber Chicken

Barbeque Spiced Turkey Mushroom Burgers

Gourmet burger variations are a great way to incorporate vegetables into a sandwich. Give this turkey version a try to satisfy your summertime barbecue craving year round.

Makes 4 servings

In a cast iron or metal skillet coated in vegetable oil, sauté the mushrooms and onions over medium heat until softened and lightly brown, set aside to cool.

Meanwhile, in a medium bowl, thoroughly combine the remaining ingredients. Divide mixture into 4 equal portions, shaping each into a 1" thick patty. Cover and refrigerate until set and firm, about 1 hour.

Recoat the same skillet with vegetable oil, heat to sizzling over medium heat. Place patties in the pan, cooking for about 5-7 minutes on each side until a golden brown crust forms, until cooked through and firm in the center, reducing heat as needed to avoid burning.

Serve on bulkie rolls if desired, with lettuce, tomato, red onion, mayonnaise and/or additional barbecue sauce.

INGREDIENTS:

vegetable oil

8 ounces baby bella or white button mushrooms, coarsely chopped

¼ cup onion, diced

¼ cup barbecue sauce

¼ cup seasoned bread crumbs

2 tablespoons spicy brown mustard

1 teaspoon chili powder

1 teaspoon smoked paprika

2 teaspoons Worcestershire sauce

½ cup fresh parsley, finely chopped

3 cloves garlic, peeled, finely minced

½ teaspoon salt

½ teaspoon freshly ground black pepper

1 pound 93% lean ground turkey

lettuce leaves, sliced tomato, sliced red onion, mayonnaise, barbeque sauce and/or bulkie rolls, if desired, to serve

Ultimate Autumn Chicken Stuffed Potatoes

A great fall meal, as colorful as peak-season leaf color. Omit the chunked chicken if you prefer a meatless main dish.

Makes 4 servings

Preheat oven to 400° F. In a small bowl, whisk thyme, red pepper flakes, garlic, vinegar, salt and pepper together until combined. Drizzle in olive oil in a stream, whisking vigorously until thoroughly combined.

In a medium bowl, combine chicken tenders and 2 tablespoons of the olive oil mixture.

On a large ungreased baking sheet, toss vegetables with remaining olive oil mixture. Spread to cover ⅔ of the baking sheet. On the remaining ⅓ of the baking sheet, place the chicken tenders. Place baking potatoes on an adjacent oven rack to the baking sheet of vegetables and bake for 25 minutes, turning the chicken tenders once during baking. Remove the chicken tenders when opaque in the center and cooked through. With a spatula, flip the vegetables. Turn over the potatoes, and continue to cook both the potato and vegetables for 20 minutes. Cook until fork tender, baking potatoes up to 15 minutes more until desired doneness.

For cheese sauce: Meanwhile, in a medium saucepan, melt butter over medium-low heat. Stir in flour to make a roux, cooking until it becomes a bubbling paste, about 2 minutes. Slowly stir in milk until combined and heated through and slightly thickened. Stir in cheeses, salt and pepper, stirring constantly until just bubbling, remove from heat immediately. May be made up to two days ahead, refrigerated in a tightly sealed container, and reheated to serve.

To serve: Cut chicken tenders into 1" chunks. Cut cooked potatoes in half lengthwise and place on serving plates, fluffing the interior with a fork. Top with equal amounts of chicken chunks and roasted vegetables. Top with cheese sauce and garnish with snipped chives, serve immediately.

INGREDIENTS:

For potatoes and chicken:

1 teaspoon dried thyme

pinch of red pepper flakes

2 cloves garlic, finely minced

1 tablespoon red wine vinegar

1 teaspoon salt

½ teaspoon freshly ground black pepper

3 tablespoons olive oil

6 chicken tenderloins

3 large carrots,
peeled and cut into ¼" thick coins

1 large Vidalia or sweet onion,
sliced into ½" wedges

1 9-ounce container fresh brussel sprouts,
halved

1 large red bell pepper, cored,
coarsely chopped

8 ounces white button mushrooms, halved

fresh chives, for garnish

For cheese sauce:

3 tablespoons butter

3 tablespoons all-purpose unbleached flour

2 cups whole or low-fat milk

¾ cup grated monterey jack
or muenster cheese

¼ cup parmesan cheese

pinch of ground red pepper

1 teaspoon salt

½ teaspoon freshly ground black pepper

Ginger Amber Chicken

Another favorite recipe resulting from a "what can I make with what I have on hand" visit to my refrigerator and cabinets. Now, knowing the taste, I make a shopping list to recreate this tasty Asian-flavored stir fry and share with gathered family and friends.

Makes 6 servings

Marinate the chicken: In a medium bowl, combine all the marinade ingredients and whisk until thoroughly incorporated. Add chicken, cover and refrigerate for 1 hour, or up to 24 hours, until dish is prepared.

Over a sink, drain the marinade from the chicken, pressing to remove all liquid. In a large wok or dutch oven, heat 1 tablespoon of oil until sizzling over medium-high heat. Carefully add the chicken, a few pieces at a time, taking caution to avoid spattering oil, stir frying all the while, until cooked through and opaque in the center. Set chicken aside.

Prepare the sauce: In a small bowl, combine all the sauce ingredients and whisk until thoroughly combined, set aside.

Prepare the stir fry: In the same wok or dutch oven, heat 2 tablespoons of vegetable or coconut oil until sizzling over medium-high heat. Reduce heat to medium, and add carrots and celery. Sauté for 2-3 minutes. Add corn, onion and mushrooms sauté for 2 more minutes, stirring constantly. Add in the water chestnuts, scallions and broccoli, stir for one minute more. Add in the sauce mixture, stirring until slightly thickened and heated through. Serve warm over rice, if desired.

INGREDIENTS:

For the marinated chicken:

2 tablespoons soy sauce or tamari sauce

2 tablespoons sweet chili sauce

1 tablespoon molasses

1 tablespoon chili garlic sauce

2 tablespoons fresh ginger, finely grated

2 cloves garlic, peeled, finely minced

1 tablespoon hoisin sauce

1 tablespoon rice wine vinegar

1 pound chicken tenders,
cut in ½" bite-size chunks

For the stir fry:

2 carrots, cut in 2" strips

2 stalks of celery, cut diagonally in ½" slices

1 ear fresh corn, stripped from the cob

½ medium onion, sliced

1 8-ounce package fresh button mushrooms,
quartered

1 8-ounce can water chestnuts, sliced,
liquid discarded

3 scallions, white and green parts chopped

1 large crown fresh broccoli, separated
into florets, steamed to fork tender

vegetable or coconut oil

For the sauce:

1 8-ounce container chicken stock

2 tablespoons dry white wine

2 tablespoons hoisin sauce

1 tablespoon soy sauce or tamari sauce

2 tablespoons fresh ginger, finely grated

1 large clove garlic, finely minced

1 teaspoon salt

½ teaspoon freshly ground black pepper

1 tablespoon cornstarch

6 servings of white or brown rice, prepared
to package directions, if desired, for serving

Chicken Saltimprese

Creativity and the kitchen go hand in hand when you think simultaneously like a home cook and an artist. My love for both classic Chicken Saltimbocca and Caprese Salad dishes resulted in this delicious "Saltimprese" main dish. It is truly an original that I think you will love, with a beautiful company-worthy presentation or the centerpiece of a special occasion. Our favorite way to enjoy this is served over a pile of fluffy mashed potatoes dressed in the pan juices.

Makes 4 servings

Prepare the chicken: On a large cutting board, between two sheets of plastic wrap or waxed paper, pound chicken tenders to ¼" thickness. In a medium bowl, whisk together garlic, olive oil, salt and pepper. Add the chicken to the marinade, refrigerate until assembly, up to 24 hours ahead.

Make the purse: On a clean dry surface or cutting board, lay out one piece of prosciutto. Cross it with a pounded chicken tender to form an X. In the center, build a stack of 1 piece of tomato, 1 piece of cheese, several onion strips and 2 basil leaves. Fold the chicken tender ends over the stack, and in the opposite direction, fold in the prosciutto ends to form a tightly sealed purse. Repeat with remaining ingredients (additional prosciutto slices can be helpful sealing in exposed ingredients). In a medium skillet, sear each purse in batches in olive oil on both sides until lightly browned. Transfer to a 9x13" glass or metal baking dish coated in cooking spray. Preheat oven to 350° F.

Prepare the sauce: In the same skillet, sauté red onion and garlic in olive oil over medium-low heat until translucent, about 2 minutes. Add in both wines, return to a simmer until reduced slightly. Add butter, lemon juice and parsley, simmer over low heat for 2 minutes. Pour the sauce over chicken purses and bake until fully cooked in the center, about 15-20 minutes. Top with shredded cheese, fresh basil, parsley, salt and pepper, and return to the oven for 5 minutes, or until the cheese begins to brown. Cut purses in half, and serve cut side up drizzled with pan juices.

INGREDIENTS:

For the chicken:

8 large chicken tenders

2 cloves of garlic, finely minced

2 tablespoons extra virgin olive oil

Salt and freshly ground black pepper to taste

For the filling and topping:

8-12 slices prosciutto

½ 8-ounce ball fresh mozzarella,
cut into 4 evenly thick slices, halved

1 large heirloom tomato, sliced,
cut to similar size as mozzarella half slices

24 fresh basil leaves, divided

1-2 slices red onion, separated into rings,
cut into 1" strips

1 cup shredded Italian blend cheese

salt and freshly ground black pepper, to taste

1 tablespoon olive oil

cooking spray

Fresh basil and parsley, finely minced,
for garnish

For the sauce:

2 tablespoons chopped red onion or shallot

2 cloves of garlic, peeled, finely minced

2 tablespoons Extra Virgin Olive Oil

1 cup Marsala wine

1 cup extra dry vermouth or dry white wine

1 tablespoon butter

1 tablespoon freshly squeezed lemon juice

½ cup fresh parsley, finely chopped

Greek Grilled Chicken

So simple, yet so versatile and tasty. Tamari or soy sauce is certainly not a usual Greek recipe ingredient, but the added color it lends makes it a worthy addition.

Makes 4 servings

In a medium bowl, combine the olive oil, wine, vermouth or water, tamari or soy sauce, lemon juice and spices. Whisk vigorously until well combined. Place chicken tenderloins in the marinade, turning several times to coat. Cover tightly and chill for 4 hours, or overnight.

Preheat a gas or charcoal grill to medium heat, grill tenderloins until they become opaque, turning once grill marks appear, cooking through on both sides. Serve with Greek Salad and Vinaigrette (page 12).

INGREDIENTS:

¼ cup Extra Virgin Olive Oil

2 tablespoons dry white wine, vermouth or water

2 cloves garlic, peeled, finely minced

1 tablespoon lemon juice,
squeezed from ½ fresh lemon

1 tablespoon tamari sauce or soy sauce

1 teaspoon dried oregano

½ teaspoon dried dill weed

½ teaspoon salt

¼ teaspoon freshly ground black pepper

8 boneless chicken tenderloins

Seafood

Grilled Ginger Orange Sea Scallops

Herb Pecan-Crusted Salmon

Gathering friends over the holidays is a great joy for a home cook and frequent host or hostess. This salmon recipe originated as the centerpiece of a serving table for a holiday party, tripled in size and served as a whole side of salmon on a platter, garnished generously with herbs and lemons. The entire fish was consumed during the party, and is now a highly requested recipe by all.

Makes 4 servings

Preheat oven to 400° F. In a small skillet, sauté butter and minced garlic over low heat until fragrant, about 3 minutes, set aside to cool.

In a medium bowl, combine lemon juice, honey and mustard until thoroughly combined. Stir in butter mixture, chopped pecans and spices.

Place salmon filet on a greased baking sheet or glass baking dish. Spread pecan mixture evenly over salmon, pressing in place. Roast uncovered for 20-25 minutes until cooked through and opaque in the center, and salmon flakes easily with a fork. Remove and discard skin by carefully separating it from the fish with a flat spatula before serving, if desired. Cut into four equal portions, serve with lemon wedges.

INGREDIENTS:

3 tablespoons butter, softened

2 small or 1 large garlic clove, finely minced

1 tablespoon freshly-squeezed lemon juice from ½ lemon

1 tablespoon honey

1 tablespoon dijon mustard

¾ cup pecans, coarsely chopped

2 tablespoons fresh parsley, finely chopped

1 tablespoon fresh dill, finely chopped, or 1½ teaspoons dried dill weed

½ teaspoon salt

½ teaspoon freshly ground black pepper

1½ pounds fresh salmon filet, skin intact

1 lemon, cut into wedges, optional, for serving

Ahi Tuna Tacos

Makes 2 servings

Dry the surface of the tuna with paper towels. Season both sides with paprika, salt and pepper. Press sesame seeds into both sides. Coat the bottom of a cast iron skillet or medium-sized fry pan with oil, and heat until sizzling over medium high heat. Sear the tuna on both sides only to medium-rare doneness, as filet will continue cooking slightly as it rests. Set aside to cool to room temperature. Chill up to 24 hours prior to serving.

Meanwhile, in a medium bowl, thoroughly combine all slaw ingredients. Refrigerate until serving, up to 24 hours.

For serving: With a very sharp knife, slice the tuna steak into ¼" thick planks. Set a soft tortilla on a dinner plate. Top with two to three slices of tuna, some slaw, guacamole and crema. Serve with fresh lime wedges and pickled jalapenos, if desired.

INGREDIENTS:

For the tuna:

1 8-ounce Ahi tuna steak, cut about 1" thick

1 tablespoon avocado or vegetable oil

1 tablespoon black (or white) sesame seeds

2 teaspoons smoked paprika

½ teaspoon salt

½ teaspoon freshly ground black pepper

For the slaw:

½ watermelon radish (or 3 regular radishes), julienne cut to matchsticks

⅓ cup fresh green cabbage, slivered

½ cup English cucumber, diced

2 teaspoons fresh squeezed lime juice

1 tablespoon avocado or vegetable oil

1 teaspoon poppy seeds

½ teaspoon onion powder

½ teaspoon salt

½ teaspoon freshly ground black pepper

For the crema: (or use store-bought)

½ cup sour cream

½ teaspoon fresh squeezed lime juice

½ teaspoon salt

heavy cream or water to thin, if needed

For serving:

homemade or store-bought medium soft flour tortillas

fresh limes

pickled jalapenos, sliced

Ultimate Guacamole (pg. 10) or use store-bought

Grilled Ginger Orange Sea Scallops

New England cooks always revel in seafood recipes, with plentiful treasures of the Atlantic Ocean nearby. Adding an Asian flair to these scallops yields nice grill marks and a little caramelization. We traditionally serve them over Apple Almond Rice (page 32) alongside fresh steamed broccoli sprinkled with sesame seeds.

Makes 4 servings

INGREDIENTS:

½ cup orange juice (with or without pulp)

¼ cup Tamari sauce or soy sauce

2 teaspoons sesame oil

1 tablespoon light brown sugar

1 tablespoon fresh ginger, finely minced

1 tablespoon fresh chives or scallions, finely sliced

½ teaspoon freshly ground black pepper

1½ pounds extra large sea scallops

In a medium bowl, combine orange juice, Tamari or soy sauce, sesame oil, brown sugar, ginger, chives or scallions and pepper. Add scallops to the bowl and turn to coat. Refrigerate for at least 30 minutes, or up to 4 hours in advance of cooking.

Heat an indoor, charcoal or gas grill to medium heat. Drain and discard the marinade from the scallops. Place the scallops on the grates, taking caution to ensure that the grate surface will prevent them from falling through.* Grill for 6-10 minutes, turning once during cooking, when grill marks appear, until the scallops are opaque and cooked through in the center. Serve hot.

*Note: *If the scallops are small in size and there is concern that they may fall through the grill grates, thread them through the center on water-soaked wood or metal skewers, taking care not to crowd them, before grilling.*

Lemon Herb Crab Cakes with Horseradish Remoulade

Vacations are often the inspiration for my recipe development creativity. On a trip to visit my parents in Myrtle Beach, South Carolina, crab cakes were all the rage at every restaurant, with the centerpiece star of crabmeat being a local delicacy. Several test run recipes and adaptations later, this star was born.

Makes 4 main course servings of 2 crab cakes, or 8 appetizers of 1 crab cake

For the remoulade: In a small bowl, thoroughly combine all remoulade ingredients. Chill covered until serving, up to 2 days.

For the crab cakes: Sauté onion in a medium pan in butter over medium-low heat until translucent and softened. Set aside to cool.

Tear bread slices into small chunks. In a blender or food processor, process until it reaches a crumb-like consistency.

In a large bowl, combine the bread crumbs with the crabmeat, egg, cream or half and half, spices, mustard, Worcestershire sauce, hot sauce and sautéed onion, tossing gently until thoroughly combined, taking care not to over mix, as the crab is best showcased intact.

Form mixture with clean hands into 8 evenly sized crab cakes and set on a plate in a single layer. Cover loosely and refrigerate for 30 minutes, or until firm.

Pour panko into a medium bowl. Carefully press each cake into the panko on both sides, return to plate.

Heat 1 tablespoon vegetable oil in a large flat non-stick or cast iron skillet. Sauté the crab cakes in small batches, leaving untouched until they turn golden brown, carefully flipping to cook both coated sides, until barely firm in the center. Serve immediately with lemon wedges and horseradish remoulade. Stays fresh for up to 3 days when refrigerated in a tightly sealed container and served at room temperature or lightly reheated.

INGREDIENTS:

Crab Cakes:

½ medium onion, finely minced

1 tablespoon butter

3 slices crusty white bread

1 pound lump fresh crab meat, drained of liquid

1 egg, beaten

2 tablespoons light cream or half and half

¼ cup fresh parsley, finely chopped

2 tablespoons fresh dill, finely chopped

½ teaspoon salt

½ teaspoon freshly ground black pepper

2 teaspoons dijon mustard
(or 1 teaspoon dry mustard)

2 teaspoons Worcestershire sauce

few dashes of hot sauce

unseasoned panko breadcrumbs

vegetable oil

2 lemons

Remoulade:

½ cup mayonnaise

1 tablespoon prepared horseradish

1 tablespoon ketchup

1 teaspoon fresh dill, finely chopped

dash of hot sauce

1 tablespoon dill relish

freshly ground black pepper to taste

Panko-Crusted Cod

In New England, cod is a preferred white soft-flesh fish common on the dinner table. If you reside in an area where it is not readily available, consider tilapia or some other mild-tasting white fish with this crusty top for an easy dinner.

Makes 2 servings

Preheat oven to 375° F. Squeeze the juice of one lemon to equal about 2 tablespoons, reserving the squeezed fruit. In a medium skillet, sauté shallot and olive oil over medium-low heat until shallot is translucent and softened. Reduce heat to low, and add in garlic and butter, stirring until melted. Add in 2 tablespoons of wine and lemon juice, stirring until combined, and remove from heat. Stir in herbs, panko, salt and pepper, set aside.

In a medium greased glass baking pan or pie plate, place cod (spaced apart if in two portions), and top with panko mixture, pressing firmly to set. Pour remaining wine into the pan surrounding the fish.

Remove fruit from the squeezed lemon and discard. Cut the remaining rind into wedges, and place in the pan. Bake for 20-25 minutes, until fish is opaque in the center. Broil 1-2 minutes more, until panko topping is crispy and brown, taking care not to burn.

Remove from the oven and serve with the caramelized lemon rind and fresh lemon wedges.

INGREDIENTS:

1 tablespoon olive oil

1 shallot, finely chopped

1 clove garlic, finely minced

3 tablespoons butter

¼ cup dry white wine, divided

2 lemons, divided

¼ cup fresh dill, finely chopped

¼ cup fresh parsley, finely chopped

½ cup seasoned panko bread crumbs

½ teaspoon salt

½ teaspoon freshly ground black pepper

¾ pound filet of fresh cod loin (cut in one or two portions)

Breads

Raspberry Walnut Coffee Ring

Cinnamon Caramel Sticky Buns

Family holidays herald this recipe, refined over many years, now a favorite breakfast here on the morning of Christmas. Consider giving the gift of fresh baked sticky buns in their partially prepared form, frozen at the last rise, and handed over to a loved one with overnight thawing and baking instructions, sharing your kitchen with others.

Makes 12 buns

For the dough: In a large bowl with a hand mixer, or the bowl of a stand mixer fitted with the dough hook, thoroughly combine 1½ cups flour, ¼ cup sugar, salt and yeast. In a small saucepan, heat 1 cup milk and ⅓ cup butter until warm (120 to 130° F, use a thermometer for accuracy). Add liquid and egg to dry ingredients, and mix on low speed until moistened. Beat for 2 minutes at medium speed. Mix in 1 cup of flour until the dough begins to pull away from the bowl.

On a floured surface, knead in remaining 1-1½ cups flour until dough is smooth and elastic, about 5 minutes. Place in a large greased bowl and cover loosely with a greased plate or lid and a cloth towel. Let rise in a warm spot until light and doubled in size, about 45 minutes.

For the topping: Grease a 9x13" glass or metal baking pan. In a small bowl, thoroughly combine butter, brown sugar and corn syrup. Drop mixture into pan and spread evenly across the bottom. Sprinkle evenly with walnuts.

With floured hands, punch down dough, removing any air bubbles, let rest for 2 minutes. On a lightly floured surface, roll the dough to a 16x12" rectangle. Brush the surface evenly with softened butter for filling. In a small bowl, combine ¼ cup sugar and 1 tablespoon cinnamon, sprinkle evenly over buttered dough. Roll tightly, starting from the long side, pressing the seam to seal. Cut into 12 uniform 1-1¼" slices, place cut side down in the greased pan. *Cover loosely with a cloth towel, and let rise in a warm spot until doubled in size, about 1 hour.

Preheat oven to 375° F. Remove towel, and bake uncovered for 25-30 minutes until golden brown, and sounds hollow when tapped. Immediately invert onto a clean flat surface or serving platter, transferring any topping left in pan to the buns. Pull buns apart and serve warm. Stays fresh up to 2 days when stored in a tightly sealed container. Serve leftover buns slightly reheated.

Note: *At this point, the pan of buns (use a tin foil pan if you wish) can be tightly covered with greased plastic wrap and then tin foil to freeze for later use or gifting. To finish, remove buns from the freezer 8-10 hours prior to baking time. Allow to rise in a warm spot until doubled in size. Remove the plastic wrap and foil before baking according to directions. For gifts, write the thawing/baking instructions on the tin foil cover.*

INGREDIENTS:

Dough:

3½-4½ cups all-purpose unbleached flour

¼ cup granulated sugar

½ teaspoon salt

1¼-ounce packet active dry yeast
(2¼ teaspoons)

1 cup whole or low-fat milk

⅓ cup butter

1 egg

Topping:

½ cup butter, softened

½ cup firmly packed light brown sugar

2 tablespoons light corn syrup

½ cup chopped walnuts

Filling:

¼ cup butter, softened

¼ cup granulated sugar

1 tablespoon ground cinnamon

Spicy Streusel Sweet Potato Oat Muffins

Makes 8 jumbo muffins, or 12-16 standard muffins

Preheat the oven to 400° F. Pierce the sweet potatoes with a fork sparsely, and roast on the center oven rack until tender, 50-60 minutes. Set aside to cool slightly, cut in half, squeeze the contents out into a medium bowl. Mash until smooth to yield about 2 cups, set aside.*

Reduce the oven temperature to 375° F. Grease with cooking spray or line muffin tins with paper baking cups (about 8 for jumbo, 12-16 for standard size tins).

In a medium bowl, whisk flour, oats, cinnamon, nutmeg, ginger, cloves, baking soda, baking powder and salt. In the bowl of a stand mixer fitted with the paddle attachment, or in a large bowl with a hand mixer, beat the eggs, mashed sweet potato, brown sugar, molasses, oil and butter until well combined. In small batches, add the dry ingredients to the wet, mixing slowly between each addition, scraping the bowl as needed with a rubber spatula, until evenly incorporated.

Prepare the streusel: Combine all ingredients in a small bowl, mixing thoroughly to combine.

Spoon the batter into the prepared muffin pans, filling each cup about ⅔ full, distributing evenly. Sprinkle the muffin tops sparsely with the streusel mixture. Bake until the muffins are golden and a toothpick inserted in a muffin comes out clean, about 20-25 minutes for standard muffins, 35-40 minutes for jumbo muffins. Remove from the oven, and cool in the pan before serving. Stays fresh when stored in a tightly sealed container for up to 3 days at room temperature, or when frozen up to 1 month.

Note: *This step can be omitted if using leftover mashed sweet potatoes in this recipe. Be sure they are at room temperature before adding to the mixture.*

INGREDIENTS:

2 medium sweet potatoes,
or 2 cups leftover mashed sweet potatoes

2¼ cups all-purpose unbleached flour

¾ cup old fashioned oats

2 teaspoons ground cinnamon

1 teaspoon ground nutmeg

½ teaspoon ground ginger

½ teaspoon ground cloves

2 teaspoons baking soda

1 teaspoon baking powder

½ teaspoon salt

3 large eggs

¾ cup light brown sugar, firmly packed

¼ cup molasses

⅓ cup vegetable oil

3 tablespoons butter, melted

cooking spray

Streusel:

3 tablespoons granulated sugar

1½ teaspoons cinnamon

½ teaspoon nutmeg

¼ teaspoon salt

¼ cup old fashioned oats

¼ cup toasted pecans, coarsely chopped

2 tablespoons butter, melted

Baked Apple Pancake

A weekend staple for my growing children, there was never a speck leftover from this fragrant, delicious confection. With a crispy "brûlée" style topping, there is no need for condiment, just slice and serve.

Makes 4 servings

Preheat the oven to 450° F. In a large skillet, melt ¼ cup butter, add apples and sauté until barely tender. Pour the mixture into a greased 9x13" glass or metal baking pan. In a medium bowl, beat eggs, milk, flour and salt, pour over the apple mixture. Bake for 15 minutes, until the pancake puffs and is partially cooked through.

Meanwhile, in a small bowl, thoroughly combine sugar and spices. Remove the pan from the oven, and drizzle the pancake with remaining ¼ cup melted butter. Sprinkle the sugar mixture evenly over the top, and bake for 5-10 minutes more, until brown and thoroughly cooked through. Turn the broiler to high, and broil until the sugar melts, watching constantly, taking care to not burn the top, about 2-3 minutes. Remove from the oven, cool slightly and cut into squares, serve immediately.

INGREDIENTS:

4 firm baking apples (Cortland or Granny Smith), peeled, thinly sliced

½ cup butter, melted, divided

6 eggs

1 cup whole or low-fat milk

1 cup all-purpose unbleached flour

½ teaspoon salt

½ cup granulated sugar

1 tablespoon ground cinnamon

1 teaspoon ground nutmeg

Cranberry Oat Breakfast Bars

My children's back to school traditions throughout their grade school years wouldn't have been complete without a double batch of these bars, keeping their on-the-go breakfasts intact. Adding ½ cup wheat germ can further fortify the protein content. Be sure to add additional milk if the addition of wheat germ makes the batter too thick.

Makes 16 bars

Preheat oven to 350° F. Spread the rolled oats evenly on an ungreased baking sheet, and toast in the oven for 12 minutes until fragrant. Set aside to cool.

In the bowl of a stand mixer fitted with the paddle attachment, or in a large bowl with a hand mixer, beat butter and brown sugar until thoroughly combined. Slowly incorporate eggs, one at a time, followed by milk and vanilla extract.

In a medium bowl, whisk together flour and spices. Blend into wet ingredients until thoroughly incorporated. Stir in cooled oats, pecans and cranberries or raisins. Spread batter into a greased 9x13" metal or glass baking pan. Bake for 25-30 minutes, until lightly browned and bars spring back when touched lightly in the center. Cool and cut into 16 bars. Stays fresh up to 4 days in a tightly sealed container, separating layers with wax paper to prevent sticking.

INGREDIENTS:

1½ cups old fashioned rolled oats

1½ sticks salted butter, softened

1 cup light brown sugar

2 large eggs

⅓ cup whole, low-fat or almond milk

2 teaspoons vanilla extract

1 cup all-purpose unbleached flour

½ teaspoon nutmeg

1 teaspoon cinnamon

½ teaspoon salt

1½ cups pecans, coarsely chopped

1¼ cups sweetened dried cranberries or raisins

Raspberry Walnut Coffee Ring

This recipe began its evolution when I was searching for pastry to mimic the appearance of a holiday wreath for the Christmas morning breakfast table. The resulting adaptation from many trial runs was a very large (think serving platter-sized) oval wreath, which no one minded! The flavor can easily be changed by selecting from your preferred variety of fruit preserves and nuts.

Makes 2 - 8" round or 1 large oval coffee ring

In a small saucepan, heat milk, 6 tablespoons butter, sugar, and salt together over medium-low heat (about 130°, use a thermometer to test for accuracy), until butter is nearly melted. Stir to blend together, remove from heat and set aside.

In the bowl of a stand mixer fitted with the dough hook, or in a large mixing bowl with a hand mixer, combine 1½ cups of flour and the yeast. Stir in milk mixture until combined, then add egg. Beat on medium-high speed for about 3 minutes, or until thoroughly combined. Stir in remaining flour, 1 cup at a time, mixing between additions. Flour hands and knead dough by hand in bowl for 2 more minutes, adding additional flour to keep your hands from sticking. Turn dough so the surface is floured, cover with an inverted greased plate or kitchen towel. Set aside until doubled in size, about 45 minutes to 1 hour.

On a floured counter surface or large wooden cutting board, punch down the dough. Roll the dough into a 12x16" rectangle. In a small bowl, combine the remaining softened butter and raspberry preserves.

Using a tablespoon or pastry brush, spread the mixture evenly across the dough surface. Sprinkle evenly with ¼ cup of the chopped walnuts. Roll the dough into a tube from the longest side, sealing the end by pinching the dough together with your fingers. With a large sharp knife, cut the tube lengthwise to form 2 half-circle ropes. With the cut side face up, twist the two dough ropes together to form a large single rope. If making two round rings, cut the rope in half at the center, yielding two ropes.

On a greased baking sheet (or in two greased 8" round baking pans), form the dough into a large oval (or two spiral circles), cover with greased plastic wrap or parchment, allow to rise in a warm place until doubled in size.

Preheat the oven to 350° F. Bake for 30-40 minutes, until the top is golden brown, and when pressed lightly in the center, the dough springs back. Cool to room temperature. Transfer to serving platter(s), if desired.

Prepare the confectioner's icing: In a small bowl, whisk powdered sugar, milk or cream and vanilla extract together until lumps disappear, adding more milk or cream to thin to a pourable consistency. Drizzle over top(s) of coffee ring(s), and sprinkle with remaining chopped walnuts.

Slice into wedges to serve. Stays fresh up to 2 days when stored at room temperature, or frozen un-iced up to one month, in a tightly sealed container. Top frozen coffee rings with icing once thawed to room temperature.

INGREDIENTS:

Coffee Ring:

1 cup milk

10 tablespoons (1¼ sticks) butter, divided

¼ cup white sugar

½ teaspoon salt

3½-4 cups unbleached all-purpose flour

1 packet (or 2¼ teaspoons) quick-rise active dry yeast

1 egg, whisked

¾ cup raspberry preserves

½ cup chopped walnuts, divided

Confectioner's Icing:

1 cup powdered sugar

1-2 tablespoons milk, half & half or cream

1 teaspoon vanilla extract

Raisin Almond Babka Braid

Having a mixed nationality background that is heavily influenced by Polish heritage inspired my exploration of yeast dough baking. This recipe is a nod to my beloved maternal grandmother, the source of many family favorite recipes, and a treasure while we enjoyed her presence in our lives. We traditionally bake this sweet bread at Easter time, make multiple batches, keeping the large round loaf for family, and sharing the standard rectangular loaves with friends. The best way to enjoy it the second day is toasting the slices, and serving topped with butter and ground cinnamon or cinnamon sugar.

Makes 1 large round babka or 2 standard loaves

In the bowl of a stand mixer with the dough hook attached, or a large bowl with a hand mixer, combine sugar, salt, yeast and 2 cups of flour. In a 2-quart saucepan, heat milk, water and butter over low heat until the butter barely melts (to about 130°, use a thermometer to test for accuracy).

Gradually beat liquid into dry ingredients over low speed. Once combined, increase speed to medium and beat for 2 minutes. Beat in 2 eggs, the egg yolk and 2 cups of flour, mixing for 2 minutes. Stir in 3-4 more cups of flour, combining thoroughly, until the dough is supple and only slightly sticky. Stir in the raisins and ½ cup almonds with a wooden spoon.

Turn the dough onto a lightly floured surface. Knead by hand until smooth and elastic, about 5 minutes. Gather the dough into a ball, and place in a large greased bowl, turning to grease the top. Cover with a tea towel, inverted greased plate or lid, and let rise in a warm place until the dough doubles, about 1-1½ hours. Punch the dough down, return to floured surface, and divide into 3 equal pieces. With floured hands, roll each piece of dough into a 20-24" rope.

Place the ropes side by side on the floured surface, and braid, pinching the ends together to seal. Coil the braid into a greased 9-10" springform pan, or cut the braid in half to form 2 loaves, and place into 2 greased loaf pans. Beat egg white with a little warm water, and brush the top and sides of the dough. Sprinkle with remaining ¼ cup sliced almonds. Cover loosely with greased wax paper and then a tea towel, and set aside to rise again in a warm place, about 30-45 minutes, until doubled.

Remove the top oven rack, placing the second in the bottom third of the oven. Preheat the oven to 350° F. Bake for 40-50 minutes for two loaves, or 60-70 minutes for the larger loaf, checking frequently to avoid overbaking. The bread is cooked through when the center springs back or sounds hollow when tapped. Cool for 10-15 minutes, remove from the pan and cool completely before slicing and serving. Stays fresh when stored in a tightly sealed bag or container for up to 3 days, freezes well for up to one month.

INGREDIENTS:

⅔ cup sugar

1 teaspoon salt

4½ teaspoons (or 2 - ½ ounce packets) active dry yeast

7-8 cups all-purpose unbleached flour

1½ cups milk

1 cup water

½ cup butter

3 eggs, divided - 1 egg separated, reserving yolk and white

1 cup raisins

¾ cup sliced almonds, divided

Sweets

Double Ginger Cookies

Pavlova Roll

Spicy Sweet Gingerbread

Memories of enjoying this at home during my own youth inspired a new variation, with plenty of extra spice to satisfy the sweet tooth of adults and children alike.

Makes 18 servings

Preheat oven to 350° F. Butter and flour a 9" square metal or glass baking pan.

In the bowl of a stand mixer fitted with the paddle attachment, or in a large bowl with a hand mixer, beat butter and sugar until fluffy and well combined. Add eggs and beat until incorporated. Carefully add boiling water, molasses and fresh ginger, stirring slowly to thoroughly blend.

In a medium bowl, whisk together the flour, baking soda, salt, ground ginger and nutmeg. In two batches, add the dry ingredients to the wet mixture, mixing until thoroughly combined. Pour into pan and bake for 40-45 minutes, or until a cake tester or toothpick inserted in the center comes out clean. Cool slightly in the pan, cut into squares to serve, topped with whipped cream if desired.

INGREDIENTS:

½ cup butter, softened

1 cup granulated sugar

2 eggs

¾ cup water, heated to boiling

¾ cup molasses

2 teaspoons fresh ginger, finely grated

2½ cups all-purpose unbleached flour

2 teaspoons baking soda

½ teaspoon salt

1 tablespoon ground ginger

1 teaspoon nutmeg

1 can spray whipped cream, to serve, optional

Spiced Apple Custard

Makes 4 servings

Place rack in top third of oven; preheat to 400° F. Generously grease a shallow 2-quart baking dish, 4 - 5" diameter ramekins, or a large pie plate with 1 tablespoon butter.

In a medium skillet, melt remaining butter and add apples, stirring until coated. Add in 2 tablespoons sugar, ¼ teaspoon salt and brandy. Sauté until apples are softened and mixture is fragrant, taking care not to burn, about 3 minutes. Set aside to cool to room temperature.

In a blender, or in a medium bowl with a whisk, blend together remaining 4 tablespoons sugar, vanilla, eggs, half and half or milk until thoroughly combined. Sprinkle the flour, spices and remaining ¾ teaspoon salt over the top, and whisk or blend until thoroughly incorporated.

Arrange apples in a single layer evenly on the bottom of the prepared baking dish or ramekins. Pour custard over the sautéed apples. Bake until puffed, golden and center is firm, about 15 minutes. Remove from the oven, sprinkle or sift powdered sugar over the surface, and return to the oven until melted and crisp, about 2-5 minutes. Allow to cool slightly before serving topped with whipped cream, if desired.

INGREDIENTS:

5 tablespoons butter, divided

6 tablespoons granulated sugar, divided

1 teaspoon salt, divided

2 large firm baking apples (Cortland or Granny Smith), peeled, cored and sliced ¼" thick

1 tablespoon brandy or apple brandy

1 teaspoon pure vanilla extract

3 large eggs

1 cup half and half, or whole milk

2 tablespoons all-purpose unbleached flour

2 teaspoons ground cinnamon

1 teaspoon ground nutmeg

2 tablespoons powdered sugar

1 can spray whipped cream, optional

Amaretto Chocolate Chip Biscotti

Somewhere along my journey with baking, I decided that biscotti were the perfect holiday season gift for neighbors and family. They bake easily in large batches, efficiently use baking sheet space, and stay fresh much longer than a traditional cookie. Though there is little possibility of Italian genes in my family tree, I have found these to be loved by every recipient, often produced by the hundreds as gift giving season approaches.

Makes about 40 biscotti

In the bowl of a stand mixer fitted with the paddle blade, or in a large bowl with a hand mixer, combine sugar and butter, beating until fluffy, about 2 minutes. Stir in the eggs, amaretto and extracts, beat on low speed until smooth, scraping the bowl as needed with a spatula.

In a medium bowl, thoroughly combine flour, baking powder and salt with a whisk. Add to the wet mixture in small batches, mixing on low speed between additions. Stir in almonds and chocolate chips with a wooden spoon, until evenly combined. Cover the bowl loosely with a lid, and chill for 30 minutes.

Grease a baking sheet with cooking spray. Preheat the oven to 350° F. Divide the chilled dough into two balls. On a floured surface, form the dough into 2 - 14" logs. Carefully set the logs side by side on the prepared baking sheet, at least 5" apart. Bake on the oven's center rack, for 30 minutes, turning the baking sheet halfway through cooking time. Remove from the oven, cool for 5 minutes.

With a large flat spatula, carefully transfer the logs to a cutting board. Cut the biscotti into ¾" thick diagonal slices. Return the slices to the baking sheet, cut side down, (a second baking sheet may be needed) and bake for 20 minutes, or until crisp and golden brown. Remove from oven, cool to room temperature. Stays fresh when stored in a tightly sealed container for up to 10 days, or freeze for up to 1 month.

INGREDIENTS:

1 cup granulated sugar

½ cup butter, softened

3 large eggs

3 tablespoon amaretto liqueur

1 teaspoon pure vanilla extract

1 teaspoon almond extract

2¾ cups all-purpose unbleached flour

1½ teaspoons baking powder

½ teaspoon salt

1 cup whole roasted salted almonds

1 cup semi-sweet chocolate chips

cooking spray

Rum-Glazed Pineapple Upside Down Cake

Pineapple makes frequent appearances in our home, especially for breakfast or in desserts, a family favorite ingredient. The rum addition to the glaze makes this a favorite among the adults.

Prepare the glaze: In a large skillet, heat butter and sugar over medium-low heat until bubbly and light brown, about 3 minutes. Add rum and cream, simmer for 4 minutes until thickened, whisking frequently, taking care not to burn the mixture. Set aside to cool.

Prepare the cake: Grease a 9" cake pan with cooking spray, line with parchment paper. Arrange pineapple rings in preferred design in the pan, together with cherries and/or pecans (if desired) in a single even layer. Top with the cooled glaze mixture, spreading evenly over the fruit design.

Preheat the oven to 350° F. In the bowl of a stand mixer fitted with the paddle attachment, or in a large bowl with a hand mixer, beat together butter and sugar until light and fluffy. Blend in egg yolks and vanilla until thoroughly combined.

In a medium bowl, combine flour, baking powder, baking soda, salt and ginger, whisk until thoroughly combined. Add dry ingredients, pineapple juice and buttermilk or curdled milk to the butter mixture alternately, beating between each addition until smooth.

In a medium bowl, whip egg whites until soft peaks form. Fold into batter in two additions. Pour the batter into the cake pan, taking care not to disrupt the fruit design. Level the batter carefully with a spatula. Bake about 1 hour, or until a cake tester or a toothpick inserted into the center comes out clean. Remove from oven, and cool for 5-10 minutes. Carefully invert onto a serving platter, taking care to avoid touching the hot caramelized topping. Serve warm. Stays fresh when stored at room temperature in a tightly sealed container up to 3 days, reheat slightly before serving.

INGREDIENTS:

Rum Glaze:

¼ cup butter

¼ cup light brown sugar

¼ cup dark rum

¼ cup light or heavy cream

Cake:

cooking spray

parchment paper

1 fresh pineapple, cored and peeled, cut into ½" thick rings

toasted pecan halves (optional)

maraschino cherries (optional)

10 tablespoons salted butter, softened

1 cup sugar

3 eggs, separated, whites and yolks reserved separately

1½ teaspoons vanilla extract

2 cups all-purpose unbleached flour

¾ teaspoon baking powder

½ teaspoon baking soda

¾ teaspoon salt

1 teaspoon ground ginger

¼ cup pineapple juice

½ cup buttermilk, or ½ cup milk combined with 1 tablespoon lemon juice until curdled

89

Chocolate Walnut Biscotti

Makes about 40 biscotti

In the bowl of a stand mixer fitted with the paddle blade, or in a large bowl with a hand mixer, combine sugar and butter, beating until fluffy, about 2 minutes. Stir in the eggs and vanilla, beat on low speed until smooth, scraping the bowl as needed with a spatula.

In a separate medium bowl, combine flour, cocoa powder, baking powder, baking soda and salt with a whisk. Add to the wet mixture in small batches, mixing on low speed between additions. Stir in walnuts and chocolate chips with a wooden spoon, until evenly combined. Cover the bowl of dough loosely with a lid, and chill for 30 minutes.

Grease a baking sheet with cooking spray. Preheat the oven to 350° F. Divide the chilled dough into two balls. On a floured surface, form the dough into 2 - 14" logs. Carefully set the logs side by side on the prepared baking sheet, at least 5" apart. Bake on the oven's center rack, for 30 minutes, turning the baking sheet halfway through cooking time. Remove from the oven, cool for 5 minutes.

With a large flat spatula, carefully transfer the logs to a cutting board. Cut the biscotti into ¾" thick diagonal slices. Return the slices to the baking sheet, cut side down, (a second baking sheet may be needed) and bake for 20 minutes, or until crisp and golden brown. Remove from oven, cool to room temperature. Stays fresh when stored in a tightly sealed container for up to 10 days, or freeze for up to 1 month.

INGREDIENTS:

1 cup granulated sugar

½ cup butter, softened

3 large eggs

1½ teaspoons vanilla extract

2¾ cups all-purpose unbleached flour

½ cup unsweetened cocoa powder

1½ teaspoons baking powder

¼ teaspoon baking soda

1 teaspoon salt

1 cup walnuts, roughly chopped

1 cup semi-sweet chocolate chips

cooking spray

Cranberry Pistachio Biscotti

Makes about 40 biscotti

In the bowl of a stand mixer fitted with the paddle blade, or in a large bowl with a hand mixer, combine sugar and butter, beating until fluffy, about 2 minutes. Stir in the eggs, extract, lemon peel and cardamom, beat on low speed until smooth, scraping the bowl as needed with a spatula.

In a separate medium bowl, combine flour, baking powder and salt with a whisk. Add to the wet mixture in small batches, mixing on low speed between additions. Stir in pistachios and cranberries with a wooden spoon, until evenly combined. Cover the bowl of dough loosely with a lid, and chill for 30 minutes.

Grease a baking sheet with cooking spray. Preheat the oven to 350° F. Divide the chilled dough into two balls. On a floured surface, form the dough into 2 - 14" logs. Carefully set the logs side by side on the prepared baking sheet, at least 5" apart. Bake on the oven's center rack, for 30 minutes, turning the baking sheet halfway through cooking time. Remove from the oven, cool for 5 minutes.

With a large flat spatula, carefully transfer the logs to a cutting board. Cut the biscotti into ¾" thick diagonal slices. Return the slices to the baking sheet, cut side down, (a second baking sheet may be needed) and bake for 20 minutes, or until crisp and golden brown. Remove from oven, cool to room temperature. Stays fresh when stored in a tightly sealed container for up to 10 days, or freeze for up to 1 month.

INGREDIENTS:

1 cup granulated sugar

½ cup butter, softened

3 large eggs

1½ teaspoons vanilla extract

1 tablespoon freshly grated lemon peel

1 teaspoon ground cardamom

2¾ cups all-purpose unbleached flour

1½ teaspoons baking powder

½ teaspoon salt

1 cup salted pistachios, shelled

1 cup sweetened dried cranberries

cooking spray

Double Ginger Cookies

My dad's favorite desserts always feature lots of spices, and these cookies are no exception. The fact that they are a namesake to our family's cat may also have influenced their widespread popularity (pictured below). The cookies also make a great freshly baked gift, and are a winner served as a sweet at a party.

Makes 28 cookies

In a medium mixing bowl whisk together flour, baking soda, ginger, cinnamon, cloves and salt until thoroughly combined, set aside.

In the bowl of a stand mixer, or a large mixing bowl with a hand mixer, blend shortening on low speed till softened. Gradually add 1 cup granulated sugar. Beat until combined, scraping sides of bowl occasionally. Beat in egg, crystalized ginger, if desired, and molasses. Slowly beat in flour mixture until thoroughly combined.

Shape dough into 1" balls. Roll balls in the coarse or demerara sugar until coated. Place 12 balls spaced evenly apart on each ungreased baking sheet, repeat with remaining dough as needed.

Bake two baking sheets at a time in a 350° F oven for 11-14 minutes or until cookies are light brown and puffed, switching racks halfway through baking. Resist overbaking to maintain chewy texture. Cool for 2 minutes and transfer cookies to a wire rack to completely cool. Stays fresh when stored in a tightly sealed container for up to 1 week, or freeze for up to 1 month.

INGREDIENTS:

2¼ cups all-purpose unbleached flour

1 teaspoon baking soda

1 tablespoon ground ginger

2 teaspoons ground cinnamon

1 teaspoon ground cloves

¼ teaspoon salt

¾ cup vegetable shortening

1 cup granulated sugar

1 egg

¼ cup molasses

½ cup crystallized ginger, finely chopped, optional

½ cup coarse or demerara sugar

Salted Toffee Almond Chocolate Shortbread Bars

Makes 18 bars

INGREDIENTS:

Shortbread Crust:

1 cup butter, softened

⅔ cup light brown sugar

2 egg yolks

1 teaspoon pure vanilla extract

⅔ cup all-purpose unbleached flour

½ teaspoon salt

Topping:

2½ cups semisweet chocolate chips

1⅓ cups salted roasted almonds, coarsely chopped

1 8-ounce bag crushed toffee bits

Preheat oven to 350° F. In the bowl of a stand mixer fitted with the paddle attachment, or in a large mixing bowl with a hand mixer, beat butter, brown sugar, egg yolks and vanilla until thoroughly combined. Thoroughly combine flour with salt, add to the butter mixture, and blend until just smooth. Grease a 9x13" glass or metal baking pan, and press in the dough so that it evenly covers the bottom of the pan. Dock the dough evenly by piercing the surface with a fork allowing the steam to escape during baking and to prevent it from bubbling. Bake for 18-22 minutes, or until the crust is light golden brown.

Remove pan from oven, sprinkle with chocolate chips, and return to the oven for 1 minute or until chips start to melt. Remove from the oven to a flat surface. Using a spatula, spread melted chocolate evenly over the crust. Sprinkle with chopped almonds and toffee bits, pressing firmly to set. Allow to cool completely before cutting into bars to serve. Stays fresh for 2 days when stored at room temperature in a tightly sealed container.

Salty Peanut Graham Cookies

For a classic campfire twist, stir in 1 cup of chopped mini marshmallows to give these cookies a s'mores spin!

Makes 36 cookies

Preheat oven to 350° F. In the bowl of a stand mixer fitted with the paddle attachment, or in a large bowl with a hand mixer, beat the butter and brown sugar until fluffy and thoroughly combined. Add the egg, and mix until incorporated. Stir in vanilla and condensed milk. Blend in peanut butter until evenly distributed.

In a medium bowl, combine flour, graham cracker crumbs, baking soda and salt. Add the dry ingredients to wet mixture in small batches, scraping the bowl with a rubber spatula as needed. Stir in chocolate chips and peanuts.

Drop the dough by heaping tablespoon-sized balls set 1" apart on greased baking sheets. Bake for 11-14 minutes until light golden brown, swapping the baking sheets between racks halfway through baking time. Cool cookies on baking sheets or racks until room temperature. Cookies stay fresh in a tightly sealed container for up to 3 days, or frozen up to 1 month.

INGREDIENTS:

½ cup butter, softened

½ cup light brown sugar

1 egg

1½ teaspoons pure vanilla extract

1 14-ounce can sweetened condensed milk

⅓ cup creamy peanut butter

1½ cups all-purpose unbleached flour

1 cup graham cracker crumbs
(pre-packaged or 14 crushed crackers)

1 teaspoon baking soda

1 teaspoon salt

2 cups semisweet or dark chocolate chips

⅔ cup salted dry roasted peanuts

Favorite Chocolate Cake

Years of creating my three children's birthday cakes provided plenty of opportunities to refine this favorite cake. The method yields a high rising and delicious result, with its rich, dark signature color.

Makes 32 servings

Preheat oven to 350° F. In a large mixing bowl with a hand mixer, or the bowl of a stand mixer fitted with the paddle blade, beat butter and shortening on medium speed until smooth, about 2 minutes. Slowly add the granulated sugar, beating until fluffy, about 2 minutes, scraping the sides of the bowl with a spatula as needed. Add cocoa powder and vanilla, and beat on medium speed about 1 more minute. With the mixer running at medium-low speed, add eggs, one at a time, beating for 1 minute between each addition. Scrape down the sides of the bowl.

In a medium bowl, whisk together flour, baking soda, baking powder and salt. Prepare the pan(s) by lightly coating with cooking spray and line the bottom with parchment paper cut to fit the pan.

Combine water and milk in a saucepan, and heat just to a simmer. Remove from heat. Add half the flour mixture and half the liquid to the butter mixture alternately, mixing and scraping the bowl between additions, combining until the batter is smooth. Divide the batter evenly between prepared pan(s), tapping the pans lightly to settle the contents.

Bake on the center oven rack until cake(s) pull slightly from the sides of the pans, and the center springs back when touched lightly. The cake is cooked through when a cake tester or toothpick inserted in the center comes out clean of crumbs, about 30-35 minutes for two pans, 35-40 minutes for a single pan. Bake for 5-10 additional minutes if necessary.

Cool cake(s) in the pan(s) for 10 minutes. Turn the cake layer(s) out, inverting onto a serving plate or baking rack to cool, if desired. Once cool, sprinkle the top with sifted powdered sugar, if desired, or frost with your favorite frosting. Slice to serve. Stays fresh when stored loosely covered at room temperature up to 2 days, or tightly wrapped and frozen up to a month.

INGREDIENTS:

½ cup butter, softened

¼ cup vegetable shortening

2 cups granulated sugar

¾ cup cocoa powder

2 teaspoons pure vanilla extract

3 large eggs

2 cups all-purpose unbleached flour

1½ teaspoons baking soda

¾ teaspoon baking powder

¾ teaspoon salt

1 cup water

½ cup whole or low-fat milk

cooking spray

½ cup powdered sugar

Equipment:

parchment paper

2 - 9" cake pans, or 1 - 9x13" glass
or non-stick rectangular baking pan

Pavlova Roll

A popular dessert in New Zealand, this version of Pavlova has all the beauty of a jelly roll, with a light and airy meringue as its star. It is best made in spring and summer when berries are fresh and in season.

Makes 8-10 servings

Preheat oven to 350° F. Line a baking sheet with parchment paper, brush the top with softened butter, set aside.

In the bowl of a stand mixer fitted with the whisk attachment, or in a large bowl with a hand mixer, beat egg whites on medium-high speed until soft peaks form, about 3 minutes. Gradually add 7 tablespoons of the sugar, beating constantly, until stiff peaks form, 1-2 more minutes. Fold cornstarch, vinegar and vanilla into whites until thoroughly incorporated. Spread the mixture onto prepared pan, keeping it from touching the sides. Sprinkle evenly with coconut and walnuts. Bake 12-15 minutes, until meringue is set and tinged with light brown edges. Remove from oven, set aside to completely cool.

In a food processor or blender, process 1 cup of the strawberries and the remaining 1 tablespoon sugar until smooth. In a medium mixing bowl, beat heavy cream until stiff peaks form.

Invert meringue onto a serving platter and carefully peel away and discard parchment. Spread whipped cream evenly over meringue, and scatter the surface with remaining strawberries and blueberries. From the long side, roll meringue in the style of a jelly roll. Garnish with strawberry purée, slice to serve. Keeps fresh for up to 4 hours when covered lightly and refrigerated until serving.

INGREDIENTS:

1 teaspoon butter, softened

4 egg whites

½ cup granulated sugar, divided

1 teaspoon cornstarch

1 teaspoon white vinegar

1 teaspoon vanilla extract

¾ cup sweetened flaked coconut

½ cup chopped walnuts

2 cups fresh strawberries, hulled and halved

2 cups fresh blueberries

1 cup heavy cream

Salted Cappuccino Blondies

A craving for a satisfying cappuccino led to the creation of its twin in a blonde brownie, a delicious and unique bar treat worth sharing.

Makes 36 squares

Preheat oven to 350° F. Grease a 9x9" metal or glass baking pan with cooking spray.

In a small saucepan, melt butter until bubbly, and lightly brown, flecked with brown bits, taking care not to burn. Remove from heat, and cool to barely warm.

In the bowl of a stand mixer fitted with the paddle attachment, or in a large bowl with a hand mixer, beat the melted butter and brown sugar, until thoroughly combined. Whisk in eggs, vanilla, espresso and water (if needed) until smooth and glossy.

In a medium bowl, whisk the espresso powder (if needed) flour, salt, baking powder, nutmeg and cinnamon until thoroughly combined. Add the dry ingredients in small batches to the butter mixture, scraping the bowl between additions, beating until smooth. Fold in walnuts.

Spread the batter in the prepared baking pan. Sprinkle sparsely with flaky sea salt, if desired. Bake until the surface is no longer shiny, cooked through when a cake tester or toothpick comes out clean when inserted in the center, about 25-35 minutes. Cool completely before cutting into 1½" squares to serve. Stays fresh when stored in a tightly sealed container at room temperature for up to 3 days, or frozen up to 1 month.

INGREDIENTS:

1 cup butter

2 cups firmly packed light brown sugar

2 eggs

1 tablespoons pure vanilla extract

2 tablespoons decaf espresso or 1 teaspoon espresso powder and 2 tablespoons water

2¼ cups all-purpose unbleached flour

½ teaspoon salt

2 teaspoons baking powder

½ teaspoon nutmeg

1½ teaspoons cinnamon

1 cup walnuts, coarsely chopped

flake-style sea salt, optional

cooking spray

Index

Index

Index

Index

Index

About the Author

As a public relations professional, home cook, fine artist and vocal musician, Michelle M. McGrath is passionate about her "life as art" approach to career, the kitchen and creative adventures. She founded McGrath PR in 2010, a niche public relations company, forging innovative marketing solutions through traditional, digital and social platforms for clients in the culture, non-profit and small business sectors. She is a devoted arts advocate, collaborating with, founding and serving on several of Massachusetts' cultural councils and arts institution committees. Her appointment as arts and entertainment correspondent was a founding facet of PACTV's PCN Community News, a premiere regional television news program on Boston's South Shore. Dovetailing her love of cooking into her career, she has enjoyed creating inventive menus and chairing several substantial social event series for regional non-profit organizations. Having raised three beloved children in her native New England region, she is now settled in the coastal community of Scituate, Massachusetts, at home in sight of the Atlantic Ocean.

Made in the USA
Middletown, DE
25 November 2020